THE JOURNEY GOES ON

Stories of Life's Adventure

Patricia Iredia

Published by

Peaches

Publications

Published in London by Peaches Publications Ltd, 2023.

www.peachespublications.co.uk

The moral right of the author has been asserted.

British Library Cataloguing in Publication Data: A catalogue record for this book is available from the British Library.

ISBN: 9798376423394.

Book cover design: Peaches Publications LTD.

Editor: Linda Green.

Typesetter: Winsome Duncan.

Proofreader: Virginia Rounding.

TABLE OF CONTENTS

DEDICATION

This book is dedicated to the late Dr Isaac Ovenseri Iredia, who was a perfect husband to me and father to our children. I wish you were here to see this outcome. You were always proud of me.

PREFACE

The journey to write this book started when the author, a widow, suddenly had too many empty hours on her hands as the children had flown the nest. Apart from the need to fill lonely gaps, she felt a compelling urge to document her experiences, past and present, around the world before the stories were forgotten. It was a kind of extended diary at conception. As she enjoyed writing, she joined a writing class to be with like-minded people and enjoyed listening to other people's stories and poetry. It was when the author was given a book with a collection of essays by her tutor, *Feel Free* by Zadie Smith, that she had her 'eureka' moment.

The author decided to put her personal collection of essays together in a book with the hope that the stories would motivate and inspire other women to look up and forward when they are feeling down. The book charts the author's journeys and encounters across different continents, her adventures and mishaps along the way, and the lessons learned.

There is a section in the book on widowhood and how to manage the complexities of life as a widow, especially with dependent children involved. She is passionate about issues that affect children so the author touches on racism and how to help Black children succeed at school and in life, despite any obstacles they may meet along the way. The author has always been interested in the variables that affect children's academic performance in school and explored this topic in her PhD thesis.

The book also includes tributes to people who have impacted the world, and the recent impacts of Brexit and the Covid-19 pandemic were not left out: the sad stories, the funny stories, and the uplifting stories are all included.

This book will empower women to be confident in their choices in life and to fulfil whatever task or projects they embark on in their own time, as life is not a race but an individual journey. Also, it gives a glimpse into what everyone can contribute to making life easier for women. Every story in the book is inspirational and demonstrates some practical solutions for navigating the highs and the lows of the journey through life.

Dr Patricia Iredia

ACKNOWLEDGEMENTS

I thank my parents, my late father and my mother, for their steadfast love and dedication to the education of their eleven daughters and one son, for which they sacrificed a lot to make it happen.

I must thank my own four daughters and one son for being the best children anyone could have: Isi Elaho, Iroghama Obasohan, Iyegbekosa Kolawole, Imade Omoregie, and Omonuwa Iredia. They have greatly supported me in every way possible to make this book a reality. I am very proud of the women and man they have become. I thank my four sons-in-law and daughter-in-law for their help and support whenever I call on them. I must mention my grandchildren here, who have motivated me to finish this book by continually reminding me that I have been talking about this book for 'a very long time, Nana'. They all encouraged me to write my book and spent time reading the different essays.

I thank my Easterhouse Writing Group for their comradeship and our tutor, Dr Jim Ferguson, for keeping the fire burning in me and helping me find my niche that made this collection of essays possible.

I thank my friend Mary Osei-Oppong who kindly read some of the stories at the beginning and made very useful suggestions and has been very encouraging throughout this journey. My thanks also go to my friend, Ms Mukami McCrum (MBE), who graciously gave her time to preview this entire book and write the Foreword for it. She also made very useful suggestions that enhanced the book.

I thank my publisher, Peaches Publications, for giving me your encouragement, expertise, and confidence to put this book out there.

FOREWORD

I am very pleased to be associated with this book written by Patricia, a sister and friend, who informed me three years ago that she was writing a book. We discussed the importance of writing and our experiences. Patricia explained that she was not writing an autobiography but a collection of essays reflecting on all aspects of life as we live it today.

I have worked with Patricia on some projects about issues that affect minority ethnic people. So, I believe she is well-placed to write about the experiences and issues concerning African women and children. The book also touches on current issues that affect everyone, such as Brexit, migration, wars and even Covid-19.

This book captures the significant aspects through the eyes of a woman called Julie, who has experienced the highs and lows of her journey, including the intrigues, prejudices, racism, mishaps, and fixes. Julie also gives heart-warming tributes to mentors and notable figures. These historical documentations are a legacy for future generations who read this book.

I was touched by the stories which resonated with my own experiences, such as keeping my tickets and receipts safe just in case I had to prove anything. One is also sharply reminded about the horrors and perils of war and what it means for the victims and humanity as a whole.

One of the stories that touched me was about how life can be made easier for widows in some African cultures by individuals and the community as a whole. This story was very insightful as it exposed some archaic 'inheritance' cultural practices that can leave women and children penniless and homeless after the demise of the patriarch in the home. One of the solutions to help widows was for men to write a will to safeguard their families when they are gone.

Another poignant theme in the book is about the racism and bullying of Black and minority ethnic people in the Western world and the effect on the development and academic success of victims, especially children. Patricia shares her experience of raising five successful children in this environment, giving some useful hints to parents, guardians, and everyone.

The book will increase understanding of the experiences of people of African origin and descent in the diaspora and those of other communities in general as reflected in every aspect of life, whether they are travelling on trains, or are at school, at work or navigating widowhood. The book adds to the many voices of people who work hard to stamp out prejudices and promote hope and commonality between all human races. I recommend this book to everyone as the stories are interesting, authentic, and told with a bit of humour, making them easy and captivating to read. Many positive episodes, such as acts of kindness from strangers and humorous moments amid serious issues, are explored in the book.

Ms Mukami McCrum MBE
Former Policy Manager
Gender Equality & Violence Against Women Team
Scottish Government Justice and Human Rights Campaigner

If you can't fly, then run,

If you can't run, then walk,

If you can't walk,

then crawl,

But whatever you do,

You have to keep

moving forward.

Martin Luther King Jr[1]

---

[1] Martin Luther King Jr, Wisdom to Inspire:
https://wisdomtoinspire.com/t/martin-luther-king-jr/4ke9wU2P/if-you-cant-fly-then-run (accessed 10 January 2023).

The Journey Continues

Chapter 1

THIS AULD HOUSE

Julie sat in her borrowed car in front of this old familiar 1960s-styled one-storey building in Benin City, Nigeria. The house was her parents' home where she had grown up. Her mum still lived there but was away for an extended stay in Philadelphia, USA, where seven of her eleven children resided. Julie looked around at the other houses up and down the street to see what changes had occurred, because there were always remarkable changes whenever she visited from abroad. Most of the original landlords had passed away, and their sons, families, or tenants now occupied the houses. Thanks to some very successful children, many homes had been demolished, and brand-new ones had sprung up in their places. Some of the landladies were still alive, like her mum, who was 91 years old, but they no longer lived there. They had dispersed to live with their children all around the world as there are no nursing homes.

Her father's house was once a bungalow but was raised to a one-storey building when she was about 5 years old as the family was expanding and it had now been re-modelled into mini flats. Julie's childhood home was in a bustling, expanding, ancient old city in West Africa called Benin City. Benin City is the capital of Edo State of Nigeria. It is situated in the Mid-Western part of Nigeria with an estimated population of about 3.5m people. Benin City is famous for its bronzes and artefacts dating back to the thirteenth century.

Benin is the centre of Nigeria's rubber industry, and oil production is a significant industry. The Nigerian Institute for Oil Palm Research (NIFOR) is in Benin City. Benin is cosmopolitan and traditional, with the centuries-old Oba's palace at the city's centre. The city centre also boasts the House of Assembly, where legislators meet, and the museum. There is a zoo on the outskirts of town and an airport. Benin is a central hub for all the states of the Federation. Many secondary schools, some of which used to be missionary schools, have been taken over by the government. Over the years, the government has slowly returned some schools to the churches, and the churches have built new schools. There are three universities in Benin City: the University of Benin, Igbinedion University and Benson Idahosa University. Julie attended the premier university of Nigeria, the University of Ibadan, in the west of the country.

Julie's family home was in 'New Benin', a newer part of the city compared to the older part around the Oba's palace. Today, Julie was visiting Benin from the UK, where she had lived for the best part of 40 years. Usually, she finds time to visit about four other houses where some of her contemporaries now live with their wives in the family homes. This second generation has become guardian angels to the remaining elderly men and women still living in their midst. In fact, one is lucky to have a young family helping to look in on one's aged mother. Many aged parents have children scattered around the country and the globe, like Julie and her siblings, who are scattered around three continents.

Julie looked up at the house with tears blurring her eyes. What was it about this old house that could bring about such strong emotions in her? She felt lost, hollow, and empty. She thought of her dad, buried at the side of the house, as she could see the headstone from the car. A glance towards the headstone and a glance up at the veranda upstairs at her dad's favourite corner, where he used to sit and survey all the goings-on in the street below, brought her childhood vividly back to life. This house was full to the brim and bustling with a father, mother, one brother, ten sisters, two cousins, an aunt, and an uncle.

All the children used to gather on the veranda outside for the 'Ibota' (midnight tales) by senior cousins who always started with 'Story, story', to which the children chanted 'story'. Some of the stories were oral history about the slave trade followed by a dirge and more stories that used to sound so far-fetched to them until they grew up and discovered that they were true, that slavery really happened. People went to the farms and never came back. Julie also heard many stories about the wicked stepmother, the clever tortoise, the hare, and the lion. All

4

these stories were delivered with great drama, with breaks into dirges and choruses in between.

This house has groomed many worthy ambassadors, Julie thought as she leaned her head back on the headrest and remembered all her sisters, brother, uncles, aunts, friends, and cousins who are now spread all over the country and the world. This morning, it was particularly poignant that her mum was not there for the first time in her life. Today, the house was occupied by strangers as part of the house had been converted into two mini flats for young families so that Julie's mum would have company in the compound. Julie was aware that she had no relative in the house, but she had felt compelled to visit as she drove past an adjacent street.

It was the strangest feeling when she had to introduce herself to the tenants as one of Mama's daughters residing abroad. She was treated with politeness and detachment, a half-smile and raised eyebrows displaying their bemusement. Julie had been born in this house. According to stories, she had even died and woken up here as a baby when she had an allergic reaction to baby formula. Julie went to school here. This house was where Julie first learned all her values and virtues. She was one of those who left at 18 for university and came back to work from home. She got married from this house.

She had very hardworking parents who did their best to provide for them. Father had a little farm in his village 30 minutes' drive away, and mum had a wee corner shop attached to the house to supplement their teaching income. Her dad owned only one house and was proud of it, while some of his mates had many houses from ill-gotten wealth, a shocking corruption by men even of that generation. There was no excuse. Life was quite simple and laid back then, but people got by on subsistence farming to supplement their 9-to-5 jobs. Families took in their extended families and housed, fed, and educated them. The pressures to be glamorous and extravagant were not so pronounced then. Life has always been poor for the poor, but it was not the poor that were corrupt but mostly the middle classes and the people in business who paid no taxes.

Most people were honest men and women, and the machinery worked, but this gradually eroded until one could hardly find a free pen or stationery in offices. Items of stationery were stolen or never bought, despite allowances being made for them. It was a far cry from the availability of all the office items when Julie started work as a civil servant in the 1970s. There appeared to be no accountability anymore, but Julie's father did not join the rat race: he was known as an honest, respectable, kind, and generous man, a father who was always proud of his children and full of compassion for all. Julie remembered him today as she stood in front of the grave.

While she was growing up, Julie's parents were teachers, and her dad became a headmaster. He was one of the few monogamous men of his time who got married in the church and stayed monogamous throughout his life. 'Baba', as he was called, was a strong disciplinarian, and proven loco parentis to all who got the opportunity to pass under his tutelage. He had some pupils whose parents sent them down to live with him to be guided in their learning and disciplined.

He was a teacher first and foremost, then a headmaster, a churchwarden and later an elected member of parliament who had a passion for helping others and fighting for social justice and the common good. Above all, he was a very loving and caring brother, husband, and father. He was a very devoted man to his immediate and extended family, which made Julie have very close uncles, aunties, and cousins, most of whom he brought up in his home.

Julie's mum was a primary school teacher as well. She spent 35 years teaching before she retired from that. Meanwhile, she never stopped striving to help provide for the family by engaging in various enterprises during the same time, such as running a groceries kiosk in front of the house where she sold sweets, soaps, beverages and so on. Julie credits the shop for her bad teeth because anytime she had to man the shop, she could not resist the temptation to chew the hard sweets very quickly before she was caught eating up all the profits! All her life, Julie's mum taught children and cared for her family, brothers and sisters-in-law, nieces, nephews, and grandchildren, which was a remarkable achievement and a huge contribution to humanity. She was always a willing babysitter for all her children who needed her. She also supported her husband throughout his teaching career and brief diversion into politics, where he won an election to the House of Assembly in 1964, through his retirement and his brief illness until he passed.

Julie thought about her mum, who was absent today. She would generally breeze in and out every day or stay for hours chatting with her, and this feeling of emptiness was not there. Now that Julie is a mother and grandmother, she always feels both pain and gratitude for her mother's sacrifices for her family. Julie's mum set very high standards for her children, and she often had to do without to feed all the mouths. Julie fixed her eyes on the spot in front of the house where her mum used to run a corner groceries shop. That spot was a hub to which many people gravitated. Could Julie imagine what it would be like when her mum was gone? No, she could not because she could feel the void of her absence at that moment, and she was only away on holiday. Julie had two sisters in town living in their own homes and she stayed with one of them while visiting, but today, nobody in their family house knew her. They were strangers, but her mum vowed to be back from America, and she eventually returned after Julie's holiday was over and she had left for the UK.

Julie sat in the car for quite a while, transfixed and unable to drive. The house she had grown up in was still standing in front of her, and people were living in it with whom she felt no connection. That day, it dawned on her that the emotion she felt was nothing to do with the physical building but rather the memories of life with her family, the magical moments of growing up, the love, tears, pain, and laughter. Julie could now identify with the sentiments of a friend she had visited just after she had lost her remaining parent when her friend had said to her (waving her hands around the living room): 'So, all this is now history.'

She thought of herself as a wife, mother and grandmother and tried to re-focus her mind on the new generation and the new memories that they are making together. Her own children have lived in different houses, in different cities, in different countries and even on three continents throughout their childhood up to adulthood, and now they own their own homes. One day, they will be left to reminisce about their early life and all the places they have lived in and visited, from Nigeria to the Middle East and different cities in the UK. As they look back on their life with their parents, the only thing that will be certain is that it will not be about the buildings or locations but about the family and all the memories they made together in all those places.

Chapter 2

THE JOURNEY GOES ON

Julie was getting ready for a trip to Stockton-on-Tees in the north of England to visit her second daughter, Ade, who lives there. Ade was planning her wedding and needed mum to help choose the gown and cake. She had made appointments with the companies for these two very important events, closely planned, so that Julie could accompany her to both. She was going to travel by train from Glasgow's Queen Street station, but the first thing that morning, she had to catch a bus from Cumbernauld in the north to Glasgow city centre, from where she would catch the train to Stockton-on-Tees in the north-east of England.

Julie is usually consumed with trepidation at the beginning of every journey which has always been a ritual for her. She goes into panic mode, tackling the preparation for travel, especially when she is going to be away for some days or weeks. From getting her tickets and gifts to organising to keep her home on the outskirts of Glasgow secure, Julie will fret every step of the way. She has a tradition of never visiting any child's home or even any home without bearing small gifts. This tradition has also been firmly ingrained in her children.

It is a lot of drama for her to embark on any journey, especially on the day of travel. She has always been in morbid fear of not hearing the alarm clock ring and missing her train, bus, or flight. Once before, Julie slept through the alarm and almost missed her ferry connection to the mainland to catch a train to London, and she could have missed her international flight that night. Also, if it were an international journey, Julie would repeatedly check that her passport and ticket were in her bag. Nowadays, the fear of forgetting one's ticket has been replaced by the fear of leaving one's phone and charger at home. E-tickets have become popular and can replace paper tickets. Julie has become so paranoid that, on one occasion, she made the taxi driver who was taking her to the airport turn back to her house as she could not locate her phone in her handbag during a panic search. By the time the taxi arrived at her front door, it turned out that the phone was inside her handbag, and if it were not for the panic, the taxi driver could have called it, but that never occurred to either of them, or he was just glad to keep the meter ticking.

This fear of missing a flight or train is always fuelled by her daughter's phone reminders ringing in her ears:

'Mom, have you checked that your phone and passport are in your bag?'

'Yes,' she replies.

'Please check it again now!' she insists. 'And don't forget the charger and adaptor.'

Despite these 'panics', Julie is an avid traveller because she loves to visit family in different parts of the world and discover new places. As she sat on the bus into the city centre, Julie's mind flashed back to some of the eventful journeys she had made in the past.

Saudi Arabia: Yanbu Al Sinaiyah

The paranoia of repeatedly checking that tickets and passports were packed started in the family when the children were little, and their mom Julie forgot their passports at their dad's base in Yanbu Al Sinaiyah in Saudi Arabia and only remembered halfway to the airport in Jeddah. Julie and the family were on their way to catch a flight back to Nigeria after their summer holiday. It was the summer of 1990. Isaac had been working in Saudi Arabia for about six months at the hospital. Julie and the children stayed behind in Nigeria and came for an extended summer holiday but had to return at the summer's end for the children to go back to school.

They could not afford to stay permanently in Saudi Arabia, which would have meant paying international school fees for two extra children because only two were covered in the contract. Therefore, the family decided to stay behind in Nigeria while the parents travelled between the two countries alternately. At that time, the idea was to save some money quickly, remain permanently in Nigeria, and not return to the UK, where the family had previously lived.

Isaac went to work for some hours on that fateful day of the return journey to Nigeria and had to rush back to take them to the airport, so it was Julie's responsibility to make sure that everything was packed and ready for the trip. They were halfway through the journey when she remembered that she had left the bag containing their passports on the dining table at 'home' in Yanbu, which resulted in their dad, Isaac, having to make a two-hour drive back home to retrieve them, and another two-hour journey back to the same spot, making it a four-hour round trip. The family have never forgotten that experience. They were lucky to have caught the flight because it was delayed. It was the time of Hajj for Nigerian pilgrims to Mecca, and Nigeria Airways was notorious for delayed flights. The flight was delayed by almost 24 hours.

Julie remembers how she had to spread dresses and wrappers on the airport floor for the children to lie on while they were waiting in the overcrowded airport veranda under the open skies. Julie had been warned that Nigeria Airways was unreliable and notorious for flight delays, so she had come prepared, especially as she was travelling with children, but she had never anticipated a 24-hour delay. However, she had woken up early that morning to cook jollof rice (a Nigerian spicy rice dish) and chicken drumsticks, and had packed apples, bananas, and drinks. They also had packets of biscuits in the hand luggage for when needed. Isaac had to go back to the car for the cooler with cold drinks as the weather was too hot to consider drinking water from a bottle without cooling it first. Buying a bottle of water at any airport was never an option for them because the price tag was always extortionate.

That journey back was also remarkable for more than the forgotten passports and flight delays. There were no coherent updates from the airline as usual, so passengers were left speculating and spreading rumours about the duration of the delay. The airport was teeming with genuine passengers, dodgy characters, and organised criminals in the guise of smooth operators – not that you could tell the difference between the good guy and the bad guy simply by looking at them. People were standing so close to each other that one could smell the sweat and breath on their faces. Everyone was holding their passports in their hands and hoping to push their way to the check-in counter to ensure their names were on the passenger list or waiting list at worst. There was no more visible orderly queue after hours of waiting around.

The chaotic scene was not helped by the mountain of luggage at their feet. Julie looked around and wondered how all that luggage would fit into the aircraft and still accommodate the combined weight of all the passengers. She was also a culprit for excessive luggage because she had four boxes of kids' bicycles and several suitcases too. Julie looked down at the stack at her feet; at that moment, another passenger exclaimed at the top of his voice that his wristwatch was missing from his wrist. It had been stolen. This incident prompted everyone to check on theirs, and Julie's husband, Isaac, discovered that he had also lost his prized wristwatch to the expert pickpockets. They could unlock wristwatches from the wrist by deliberately brushing their body against yours in the crowded airport to undo the clasps.

Some of the children's new shoes were also lost as they had taken them off to lie down on the airport veranda. Julie suspected the cleaners had 'swept' them away as they dozed outside. They were lucky that they had other shoes in their suitcases to put on. Isaac was always inside, keeping an eye on their belongings and watching for updates on the flight. Julie could breathe a sigh of relief when she was sitting on the plane and the plane took off. What an eventful 24 hours it had been, just as the whole holiday trip had been eventful, in other ways, right from the start of the journey in Nigeria and during the visit to Saudi Arabia.

This holiday was Julie's first visit with the children to Yanbu. Saudi Arabia was an amazing place to visit. In Jeddah and the towns and cities, one could see how a desert landscape was turned into an oasis with palm trees lining the routes and sprinklers timed to water the plants in spectacular displays. The local food was an amazing variety of spicy and aromatic cuisine, and the generosity of the Indigenes was second to none. When their neighbours, co-workers and friends of Isaac's heard that his family were visiting, they ordered food to be sent to the house. The food arrived on very large wide-brimmed silver trays. It was quite a variety of food with rice, potatoes, vegetables, and assorted meat, cooked with cloves, currants, and spices. There were about eight whole chickens and beef, oxtail, and tripe around the tray; the trays were wide enough for many people to sit around and eat together, and this was the local tradition.

The food was so much that Isaac took some to work for his sister-in-law to take to the female accommodation and share with others. Julie's sister, Angela, worked as a pharmacist at the same hospital and lived in shared accommodation in a huge block of flats for women employees of the government. However, she could not come to visit her sister or brother-in-law and their children without an official permit which had to be applied for. The food was so much that there was no time to get an official permit; hence he had to take the food to her at the hospital at closing time. It felt good to share the food with other people.

At that time, many other Nigerian men and women worked in Yanbu as doctors, nurses, physiotherapists, and medical records staff. Julie remembers when Isaac hosted the Nigerians to visit his family and when he hosted a birthday party for Angela. Isaac had to apply for a special permit for both events. The Nigerians' visit to her family was very different from the birthday party. At the first party, the Nigerian ladies and gentlemen brought in all the food and drinks to welcome Julie and the children, but Isaac decided to cater alone at the birthday party and show off his culinary skills. He prepared all the food alone, but the showing-off came at a price when he suffered repetitive strain injury to his palm and fingers from chopping lots of vegetables. This injury was a little concerning for someone who needed his hands for surgery.

Luckily, he was left-handed when handling the surgical instruments for operations. His ambidextrous skill was the saving grace because it took quite a while for the right hand to heal and return to full normal function. Isaac felt it was all worth it because everyone enjoyed the party, especially being far away from home and spending time with other Africans. The family also got to spend time with the locals and got some invites to visit their homes. On that journey, Julie also learnt some Indian curry recipes from the lady doctor who was their neighbour.

There was a lot to see and do in Yanbu. The shops were packed full of children's occasion clothes. Back home in Benin City, Sunday best for kids were 'bonfo' dresses for girls and suits for boys, depending on the home. Some homes were more traditional, so some children wore African print material. 'Bonfo' dresses were dresses with underskirts and were very dressy. It seems a little formal, but those were the choice outfits for Sunday best, birthday parties and weddings for Julie's children. There was a huge array of choices in the shops for women who liked scarves, glitter tops, and long dresses. The selection of Arabian oily perfumes in tiny bottles was very potent and plentiful. The gold market was street after street of glitter, adorning window displays, show cabinets, and even draped on the shop walls. Gold jewellery was on display everywhere. Shopping was only possible in the evenings and night time as it was just too hot during the day. It was the same with the parks near the house where children could play in the evenings and at night.

The most noticeable things were the mosques, all sparkling white and beautiful. Julie always wondered if a special ingredient made white look whiter on the buildings. It was quite admirable to observe the devotion of their prayer routines and especially the selfless commitment to the common good, and the lack of open corruption was obvious. Their projects were executed to very high standards, as misappropriating the contract funds was not an option. There was a very deep sense of responsibility and community spirit. No one would think of embezzling money for projects meant for the greater good of all.

Many people always asked Julie if she had to wear the 'abaya', the long black dress, some with a face cover. The dress code for the ladies was not so strict when Julie visited. All that was required then was adequate coverage and decency. One was okay with any outfit so long as it was loose-fitting; the sleeve of the blouse should be at least three-quarter length, with a long skirt or wrapper, and a head tie. Foreign visitors were not forced to cover their faces or wear gloves in Yanbu Al Sinaiyah, but they heard stories that some regions enforced the rule then, but Julie could not verify that. Yanbu Al Sinaiyah was a purpose-built new town and very cosmopolitan, but everyone respected and obeyed the local traditions, and there were no problems if one did that.

The children enjoyed all the places of attraction like the amusement parks and the zoo but especially the daily trips to the ice cream parlour. One 5-year-old child enjoyed the ice cream trips with her dad so much that she made a dramatic impromptu declaration: 'If mummy and daddy quarrel and decide to go their separate ways, and they both say, "I want my children", me, I will go with my daddy.' Daddy was chuffed and flabbergasted at the same time. Who would have thought that discussion around them about their auntie's messy divorce at the time had had any impact on the children? One cannot be too careful when talking in the presence of children.

Julie sighed with nostalgia as she thought about those long-ago days and eventful journeys with five young children in tow, beginning when they set foot out of the house in Benin City towards the first leg of the journey out of the country.

Benin City to Lagos

Travelling from Benin City to Lagos in Nigeria to catch an international flight was daunting. One must navigate the road's physical difficulties, especially following heavy rainfall and the real fear of highway robbers. The situation was further exacerbated as there were treacherous trenches in the middle of the road due to negligence and corruption, poor road maintenance and contractors who were more concerned with money-making than with doing a good repair job.

One could safely say that, 30 years later, the road remains very dangerous to navigate, both in terms of the treacherous trenches on the roads and highway robbers. You just never know what might happen. The journey should take about four hours if all is well. Fear and trepidation make it a most difficult journey because even the thought of embarking on the travel causes anxiety. There have been too many stories of armed robberies, accidents, and gridlock, causing people to miss their flights, etc. One finds oneself becoming very prayerful and saying daily rosaries for divine protection on that road. On a day when the roads are good, the journey is a maximum of four hours, but the roads are often only good for one dry season at a time because once the rains come, the poor repair breaks down again, and we are back to treacherous trenches. The asphalt is washed away by the early rains, and the resulting huge potholes are back. Every holiday presented new obstacles in the journey.

These obstacles were because of bungled road contracts and corrupt politicians. Money allocated for road maintenance and other public services was usually embezzled and shared between corrupt politicians and contractors. For almost a decade, there was a bad spot in Ore, one of the towns between the south and Lagos. That section of the road was so bad that a usual three-minute journey through the spot took between three and six hours, depending on whether it was raining and how stuck you got because of road damage, traffic and accidents. There was a large gully on that road. The delay was so long that the spot became a bustling market where hawkers could sell their wares, weaving between the cars, and street food vendors set up kiosks on the sides to sell hot food and snacks. Vehicles could be seen diverting into dusty or muddy side streets, trying to circumvent the bad spot, but the story was the same, no matter what route you tried to take. Julie had experienced this for three years while at the University of Ibadan in the 70s and had to pass through there regularly.

Some in the government ignored this situation for years because their focus was on setting up their own private domestic airline businesses, so it was advantageous to have bad roads, especially the Benin-Lagos Road, which was one of the busiest hubs in the country. Benin is a central location to most places; these airlines would be profitable if people chose them over travelling by road. Unfortunately, not everyone could afford the airfares and not every type of cargo lent itself to air travel, and not every destination had an airport. It was a common sight then to see lorries with fresh food stuck in the heat for hours, and one could smell the baskets of rotting tomatoes destined for the markets, which were by now pouring their juices along the route. The government eventually filled the long deep hole at the centre of the road, but the issue of road maintenance persists.

The road remained notorious for uncertainty. An accident on the road could keep cars gridlocked for hours without any visible road traffic officers to clear the road. Sometimes, the drivers and passengers would come out and try to help. Still, some unscrupulous drivers would not let other cars or lorries go before their lane for fear of being blocked again. It always deteriorated into shouting and fighting each other. It could be in the dead heat, and everyone was sweating profusely. Even if you had air conditioning in your car, there was the worry of using up all the petrol, so engines were usually switched off. Sometimes, a military officer, police officer, or politician came along, accompanied by armed guards in a truck, blaring their horns and sirens. Jumping out of their vehicles, they waved guns, cleared the way for their boss to pass through, and left the chaos behind.

On the road, people suffered all that, and in addition, they worried about service station stops for fear of attracting the attention of robbers or being followed and attacked on the highway. Most private cars would rather not stop, if possible, but people sometimes needed comfort breaks. One could garner unsavoury attention from undesirable people just by stopping at service stations. Julie remembers past stops where one noticed so many dodgy-looking fellows burrowing their eyes into yours. At times like those, she avoided eye contact to avoid drawing attention to herself or aggravating anybody.

Julie used to strip herself of any jewellery or item that could show affluence or attract attention. She always travelled that route in an African caftan dress with her hair covered to avoid getting dust in her hair, and only changed to trousers and tops in the airport toilets. That was on a day that she went straight to the airport to catch a night flight. It was better to dumb down and blend in fully than look like you were carrying a foreign passport and heading for the airport. During the time of year when the roads were awful, it was safer to travel to Lagos the day before the international flight to avoid missing the flight. One heavy rain could cause traffic disruption for hours on the roads.

Thankfully, road conditions have improved in recent years, and the roads are full of armed traffic officers and special forces at various checkpoints to protect the public from highway robbers. Still, the reality is that they cannot patrol every stretch of the road. It must be said that most travellers like Julie are very paranoid and tend to forget that there is crime in every country. The lack of trust in the government to keep one safe fuels the accumulated and sometimes irrational fear of others.

Nowadays, there is the new threat of alleged Fulani herdsmen (nomads) jumping out of bushes to attack and kidnap travellers. Kidnapping is a new danger warping the sense of normality and causing outrage amongst the populace. The highway police are expected to save travellers from these kidnappers, but the reality is that, sometimes, the police may not be as well equipped as these robbers. However, Julie felt safer when there were many police checkpoints on the road. Nowadays, the checkpoints between Benin and Lagos help make one feel safer on the roads. One can also be spared all the hassle on the roads by simply flying where possible, but one must still be conscious of flight delays when planning the journey because every little change in weather affects flights.

After the stress of the road journey, one got to the airport and met another drama. Those were the days in the 70s when you had to know somebody and make arrangements with them before going to the airport. The whole point was that your contact would help you get a boarding pass for the flight. One arrived to meet a huge crowd in the departure lounge, comprised of travellers, relatives, escorts, touts, traders, and airport officials. The touts would harass everyone, soliciting for business, from selling currency to hooking one up with an officer and so on. The traders would sell you anything from duct tape to trolley bags. The relatives would come along to help secure a boarding pass, especially if the traveller was a woman with kids. The women and kids stayed in a corner while the men ran around trying to identify a helper or using brute force to get ahead of others, even if it meant climbing over them. There were no queues in those days, or rather people refused to follow the queue; it was simply a shouting and fighting match. Some passengers had their clothes torn in the struggle to reach the check-in desk, some resorted to physical fights, and all the while with hands stretched out with their passports pointing towards the check-in desk. It was always a survival-of-the-fittest fight.

Meanwhile, there was blatant corruption going on for all to see. Some officials in uniform were openly collecting bribes to get one on the flight; it did not matter whether one had a confirmed ticket or not. Sometimes, touts came to you offering their services for the payment of a fee, claiming to be working on behalf of the official agents. You had to decide whether to trust them with your passports to get them stamped for travel. There were notices all over the airport advising travellers against giving passports to touts, but some desperate or gullible people still took the risk. Some were lucky and got away with it, while others lost their passports and money to con men. Flights were sometimes over-booked, so you could be left behind even with a confirmed ticket. If you are wondering what happened after you successfully got on the flight, the truth is shocking. Most times, the flight was not even half-full, which meant that all that fighting was orchestrated to create artificial scarcity so the officers on duty could make money.

It is good to note that things have improved in later years to a normal situation by international standards at check-in counters at the airport, but one cannot, and must not, forget how it used to be to keep us on our toes.

London to Lagos

Those were the days when travelling with Nigeria Airways through Heathrow Airport was a nightmare. Their check-in area used to be cordoned off with thick ropes to contain Nigeria Airways passengers and their huge mountains of luggage. Rumour had it then that officials tolerated the chaotic situation because Nigerians were bringing a lot of money into the country. They loved to travel and shop, so they brought in a lot of money, and there were no travel restrictions on Nigerians then, so they came in their droves. Some of the airlines had two flights daily to and from Nigeria. Nigeria was going through the oil-boom days, and some Nigerians would rather buy all their groceries from London at that time. Julie witnessed her friend fill a suitcase with 5kg bags of onions and spices in London because Christmas was approaching, and onions were expensive at that time in Nigeria, she said. Well, this was not so cheap when one considered the cost of the excess luggage that they were prepared to pay to import those items.

It was a bit saner than the chaos at Lagos Airport then but only in terms of the shouting and fighting. However, it was still the loudest and most chaotic check-in desk that drew the attention of other passengers at Heathrow. The officials there also practised the corrupt behaviours they had brought from Nigeria. To be posted to the London Branch of Nigeria Airways meant you had 'made it'. Julie remembers searching for 'who knows who' before going to the airport. Sometimes one would arm oneself with a note from a significant person, a politician, businessman or friend, introducing you to the manager or officials they knew.

Julie sometimes wondered if the white British officials working with them were complicit in all the dodgy business or if they just turned a blind eye. On reflection also, how dangerous it was to record false weights on suitcases which could have led to the overloading of the aircraft. Those were the dark days in the history of

Nigeria Airways. It is no wonder it did not survive the mismanagement and eventually collapsed. The 'giant' of Africa was left without an airline of her own to this day. The airline missed out on an excellent opportunity to be commercially viable because this was a time when Nigerians travelled to London a lot. In fact, many Nigerians treated London like a second home at that time.

Holiday job in London

In the 1970s, Julie was an undergraduate at the University of Ibadan and spent a summer holiday working in London, like most of her peers. The first time she came to London, in 1977, she stayed in south-west London with her uncle's girlfriend, who lived in a council flat near Brixton Road. She offered Julie her spare bedroom for the summer. Julie had travelled with some friends from the university, and one of them and her cousin went home with Julie when their expected host did not come to pick them up from Heathrow Airport. They promised they would find their way to another destination the next day. Aunty Bibi was very kind to accept them even though the flat had only two bedrooms. She worked as a care assistant and was going on night duty at the nursing home for the next two weeks, so she said Julie could sleep in her bedroom while the guests could use the spare room.

They would have been happy to sleep on the floor all night if they had to. Luckily, they did not have to. Aunty Bibi said they could stay for as long as they wished if they were stranded. At this point, Julie's friends were still hoping to connect with their host. Julie figured Aunty was relieved that she had company and did not have to feel guilty for 'abandoning' her. Her friends were very grateful for the accommodation and Julie was very happy to have the company of her mates for a few days. Julie had planned to meet with some other friends, but it was even better that she had people with her to explore with.

One of the girls had come to London before, so they were lucky to have her as a guide. In the morning, at 5.00 a.m., they took a bus to the corner of Bond Street, where they met many other casual workers waiting to be picked up by the agents who had jobs for them. This job was perfect because one did not need a bank account. The pay was cash-in-hand, and one could not complain that it was slightly below the average for London. Some people were taken to a hotel to work as chambermaids. Aunty warned Julie against that job because of the experiences of some of her friends who had done it. They said it was challenging because they were given too many beds to make which caused severe back pain, as it was hard to stand upright after bending to make beds all day. Julie refused to join that group.

The agent now offered them another job cleaning offices. Her friends accepted that, but she refused because she felt they were keeping the best for last. Julie took a risk because they may not have needed catering assistants on the day. Aunty said the best job, if she could get it, was catering, as one got to eat as much as one wanted when working in a kitchen. Students liked to save all their money for shopping and school expenses and not on expensive food.

Julie joined the group taken to the big post office at King's Cross. It had a big cafeteria that sold snacks and lunch to the post office staff. Julie was assigned to the drinks machine and selling snacks on the counter. Her duties included selling tea, coffee, soft drinks, and snacks, including sandwiches, cleaning, and mopping. She had to find time to top up the big dispensers of orange and cola drinks, a mixture of powder and water from the taps served in glasses. Customers could buy canned drinks if they preferred that. There were quiet moments, but one had to use the time to clean up and arrange more snacks for sale.

The breaks for the workers were staggered, but a huge influx came in at lunchtime, and it was quite challenging to multitask without looking flustered. She had been well drilled by her friends who had done that job before. Julie had to claim that she had experience of doing that job before being hired. The first day was tough as she was not used to standing for seven hours at a stretch with an hour's break. Sometimes she felt as if she was going to faint.

Julie was so flustered from juggling the job that she kept downing cold soft drinks to cool down. She could not believe she could drink as much soda from the dispenser as she wanted, but she was not allowed to take the canned drinks. During her break, Julie ate the hot food of her choice from the canteen. Julie had drunk so much mineral water that she had diarrhoea by the evening when she got home. She struggled to get up in the morning to go to work but needed the job. From then on, Julie never tasted soft drinks again; she drank only water. She considered herself lucky to get free hot lunches during her break and to have the same job for four weeks. Someone may have been on holiday, not just having a day off. The staff liked her work, or she would have been replaced.

One of the sad things she observed was the difference in the buying power of the white staff and the ethnic minority staff. The difference was so glaring that it left her wondering why the Black people could not buy themselves proper lunch. Some looked hungry but always bought very little and avoided eye contact, almost as if they were embarrassed. Were they spreading their salary too thin with extended family in Africa, or were they just like her, needing to save money on food? It does not matter what the reasons were; what was evident was that they needed to save money.

Something happened between Julie and her guests that left her so traumatised that she feels the pain to this day. Having rescued them at the airport and taken them home to her aunt's place, they became really good companions. They would watch films together in the evenings and even explored the markets together on days off. There was no more talk about when they intended to move to their original host whom they had reconnected with. In those days, there were no mobile phones, so communication was not so easy. It was public phones and landlines. One could receive calls with permission but could not use someone else's phone to make calls.

One day, Julie noticed that the girls were very agitated and were turning their room upside down searching for something. Julie asked what the problem was, and they said it was nothing. Soon after, they left very suddenly and unceremoniously without any explanation, taking all their belongings with them. They simply packed up and left. Julie was left in shock and when her Aunty got back from work, she too was very surprised. Her Aunty said she had experienced ingratitude before but not of this scale. Julie was so devastated that it was like a bereavement. She had to go searching for her other friends that she had abandoned on this visit.

Julie remains grateful to God for what transpired later. It was about two months after they got back to the university that Julie found out what had happened in London. Her friend had the grace to confess to her that they thought their money had been stolen but it was later found hidden inside their coat pocket! Julie remembers bursting into tears at the thought that she was considered a thief. What fickle trust and what ingratitude. If she had been told, she might have found the money if she had joined in the search. Their search was clouded by suspicion, so they did not do a proper search and missed the most obvious places to look. This incident happened in 1977 and Julie is still traumatised by it.

Julie was not very streetwise and got caught twice in two days when she let her guard down while shopping in London. She had been warned about there being many pickpockets in London and still got caught. It was a sad day when she lost all her Marks and Spencer shopping in the Brick Lane market. She had spent a lot of money to buy toiletries, nighties, and underwear because Marks and Spencer were quite reputable for durability and comfort, so it was an investment to last a while. While in the market, she stopped at a shed selling ladies' clothes. The dresses looked beautiful, and the prices were very attractive. There was a big placard stating, 'Buy one, get one free'. They had a few samples hanging from the roof and sides of the tent and lots more arranged on the table, which customers could pick up for a closer look.

In a moment of excitement, Julie put her shopping bags on the ground next to her feet to free her hands because the bags were quite heavy. A few minutes later, she had a few dresses paid for and decided to pick up her Marks and Spencer bags to put the dresses inside, but they were gone and replaced by a bag of rubbish touching her leg. Julie was devastated because she had spent all her money and was returning home in two days. Fortunately, her uncle came to visit in the evening and gave her 50 pounds as a gift because Aunty must have told him about her loss. Only when she was older did she realise that that was a very kind gesture.

Julie had a weekly bus pass which allowed her to jump in and out of buses for the whole day, and it was due to expire on her last day. Julie returned to Oxford Street M&S to replace some of her losses. She had kept a £20 note aside for gifts, as it was unthinkable to return home without any gifts for her friends. She had decided to return for some lavender and magnolia toiletries like soaps, deodorants, and powder sets on sale. The big shops on Oxford Street had better sales and more variety than her local shops. It was amazing to get as many as ten gift sets for less than £20, as they were half-price for £1.99 each. Julie selected her nighties and underwear and paid for them before going upstairs for the toiletries on sale near a cashier till close to a lift. Julie joined the queue.

There was only one elderly lady in front of her, maybe in her eighties, putting her stuff on the counter. Julie went to the other cashier and put her packets of toiletries on the table with her £20 note, clearly visible on the side. She could not be bothered to pick up the money as she had been holding the note in her hands to save time from opening her handbag again. Besides, she was holding shopping bags in her hands, too petrified to put them down. As Julie put her stuff on the counter, the cashier gestured to her to use the other cashier as there was only the old lady there. She then pushed her stuff towards the other cashier, who was still attending to the elderly lady. Julie was confused because she did get a nod to come forward. Julie then politely went back to queue behind the old lady while waiting to be served. Meanwhile, she became distracted by admiring all the sales goods arranged nearby and wishing she had more money to buy more gifts and had forgotten entirely about her money.

The old lady finished her transaction, turned to leave, and was about to enter the lift when Julie stepped before the cashier and realised her £20 note was gone. She instinctively looked towards the old lady who was disappearing into the lift. She raised the alarm that her money had disappeared, but no one could help her even though the manager was called, and they all made the right noises. Her money had disappeared between the three ladies, but which one of them? She wished the other cashier had attended to her; this would not have happened because she would have been right there, keeping an eye on her stuff. Did the first cashier take the money, believing that Julie did not know it was there? Was that why she pushed her stuff to the second cashier and left the scene? She will never know the answer to that. It was shocking to her because that was her second loss in two consecutive days. It was unthinkable not to have any gifts for friends, no matter how little. No one would believe her story, so the solution was to open her shopping bags and return some of the nightdresses and underwear that she had just purchased.

Julie was shocked that people would steal in the open market and inside the shop. She had no proof that the old lady took the money because she was not watching all the time, it only just seemed so, but one has watched enough detective films and documentaries to know that the culprit is not always the one who looks the most suspicious. There was nothing Julie could have done as she could not accuse anyone of stealing the money nor could she demand an investigation that involved CCTV for £20, even though that was a lot of money for a student on a summer job 45 years ago. It was foolish and careless to place her money on the counter before it was time to pay her bill. Julie counted her losses and rushed home to prepare for the airport a few hours later. She felt so foolish at what happened that she did not tell her Aunty about it until 30 years later when they were reminiscing about the good old days.

Glasgow to Philadelphia

Over the years, Nigerians soon shifted their attention to America. Despite London still being their favourite place, many families are now sending their children to the United States for education as international students. Everyone seemed to be heading there for the holidays; it suddenly became desirable. Eventually, it became the number one holiday destination for travellers. The reasons for this shift were myriad: the shopping experience, a shift in perception of what was posh or proper, more job opportunities, a style of schooling that was more flexible, and more family connections. Julie started living in the UK while all her family were in Nigeria. Eventually (over 30 years ago), some of her sisters won settlement visas to settle in the USA. Today, Julie has six sisters and a brother in the US. Julie's family base became Philadelphia in the United States, when her mother resided there for a couple of years with her older sister. Julie, too, became a frequent visitor to the US.

Philadelphia was an old city with a dated airport compared to the new sleek airports Julie had flown through in recent years. Julie became a frequent visitor for nieces' and nephews' weddings, big birthday parties, or just visiting on holiday to catch up with family. The shopping experience was second to none, especially visiting the out-of-town outlet malls with huge discounts. There was also plenty of food with 'huge' portions compared to what one was used to in the United Kingdom. Julie found the breakfast cafes particularly fascinating for the quantity of food eaten for breakfast.

On one visit to the United States in 2008, Julie, her daughter, and grandson joined the rest of the family on the holiday of a lifetime to Disney World in Florida. Disney World lived up to its hype for the sheer variety of shows, rides, food, scenery, etc. The visit to Kissimmee, Orlando, and other cities was one of the highlights of visiting Walt Disney World Resort. Julie was glad she had tagged along to be the babysitter for the kids while the more adventurous ones went on wild rides in the park.

Glasgow to Stockton

Julie's mind returned sharply to the present. Enough of reminiscing about past travels and past life events, she chided herself. It was like an out-of-body experience just sitting there staring blankly ahead while reliving the past. Today's journey was a train from Glasgow city centre to Stockton-on-Tees in the north of England. She got the 7.05 a.m. X3 bus from Cumbernauld to Queen Street train station, and the journey took about an hour on the bus. Looking at the crush at the train station, Julie was happy to be spared the hassle of hustling for a seat later when she got on the train because she always reserved a seat and arrived early for her train. This morning, the temperature was cool, but her daughter had advised her to put extra jumpers in her suitcase just in case it got colder later in the day. On arrival at the platform area at the train station, the weather had turned chilly, which seemed like a cold snap. Julie noticed that some passengers had started to put on the coats they had tied around their waists. The first thing she did on arrival was to look urgently around for the toilet as she rushed past the crowd in the waiting area to the toilet to open her suitcase and put on more layers.

What a surprise it was, or perhaps not a surprise, that a security guard entered the toilet to check her out. She was the only other African person Julie saw downstairs, wearing a bright yellow Scottish Rail waistcoat and sitting behind a little kiosk. Julie has become very adept at playing dumb. Age does that to one. She wondered what excuse she would come up with for following her into the toilet. Julie was not surprised to be noticed because she always has an oversized suitcase which attracts attention. The toilet suite was huge and empty with a row of wash-hand basins and mirrors, including half a wall of standing mirrors. There were also signs for the washrooms and rows of toilets. Julie could not be bothered about privacy as she opened her suitcase in full view of her 'guest' who smiled at her and made no attempt at excuses. She asked,

'Where are you off to today?'

'I'm on the way to Stockton to see my daughter,' answered Julie.

She just stood there without even pretending that she had come into the toilet to use it and all the time staring at the suitcase Julie had left wide open with some of its contents scattered on the floor. They struck up a conversation, and Julie noticed the name on her badge, and what a weird coincidence that her surname was the same as Julie's daughter's married name from a Nigerian tribe. Were they related? Further probing established that they were unrelated; it was a common name across a broad region. Julie took out her warm jumper and thick cardigan and put them on while holding a conversation. Julie told her about how her suitcase flew across the aisle, straight into her legs at the reserved seats for the disabled. It was as if there was a magnetic connection on the bus. It was hilarious.

Julie left the suitcase under her care to go into the toilet, which she did not need but was determined to use the 30p she had paid to get in. On returning from the toilet, Julie noticed her suitcase had been rummaged through, probably to determine its contents, or perhaps she imagined it. A yellow shirt Julie remembered hanging out down the side of the suitcase was no longer showing on her return. Julie felt amused at her antics and the fact that the guard never said why she had left her duty post and come into the toilet or why she was on the phone most of the time texting. Was she giving reports, or was she skiving off work? She had probably quickly determined that this aged woman was no threat of any sort and had decided to extend her detective work a bit longer than was necessary. Julie is a sucker for correctness. With the threat of random terrorist attacks and heightened security concerns, Julie never minds scrutiny and searches at borders so long as they are done with respect and with dignity. She values her safety and the safety of all other passengers.

The drama of that morning was just beginning. Julie's daughter was right to keep reminding her to check her travel papers. She usually has a habit of mentioning every item by name, but it turned out that she did not mention the 'Senior Railcard', and Julie had mistakenly removed it from her purse while decluttering it. She needed to make her bag lighter because she suffers from spondylosis which makes her bones ache when she carries anything heavy. Julie was about to pass through the barriers to the trains but could not find the Senior Railcard in her purse. She mentioned it to an officer at the gate, who advised her to purchase another ticket. The standard day ticket would have cost 84 pounds.

Thank God she had time to ponder the situation and make her decision.

Julie rushed to the ticket office to explain that she had a ticket, which had cost her only 19 pounds, 50 pence (£19.50) but had no railcard to go with it. The lady at the counter then advised her to buy another Senior Railcard rather than another ticket. It was a brilliant solution because she got to keep her original discounted ticket and gain an eight extra months on the new Senior Railcard. One big lesson from this carry-on was always to be early for events or travel to make room for any eventualities.

Julie could only imagine the scene, rushing into the carriage without a railcard; the possibilities swirled in her mind, the indignity and humiliation of being thrown out of the carriage or being made to buy a full standard ticket. She reckoned that, if she had taken her chance and got on the train, the cost to her would have been more than the monetary implication; it would have been an embarrassment to herself and her race. Julie always feels that she bears responsibility to her race to always stay on the right path, as any offence committed by her may be generalised to 'everyone' like her. That is one problem of being an ethnic minority person. You lose the right to be judged as an individual. It would be something like, 'Here they come again.'

Julie wonders why she always gets into these situations. It is no wonder then that her daughter is always on her case, especially as she herself is the one who narrates the stories to her family after they happen. Julie once narrated her experience of using an outdated ticket on a train journey. Her daughter in Manchester had just had a new baby, and Julie was travelling to see her and help with the baby for some time. In Nigeria, this is called 'omugwo', which translates as going to help a new mum out. Traditionally, the mother was supposed to return home with plenty of gifts after giving the help. Nowadays, the mother bears gifts, does all the hard work to help, and is lucky to get a train ticket.

The baby decided to arrive early on the day planned for the baby shower. The pre-ordered food was wasted when the event was cancelled. Guests had to be notified not to show up. The baby came early, which was why Julie had not prepared to travel at that time. Julie arrived promptly in Manchester, but after one week, she went back home for the weekend to attend an important event of the African Caribbean Women's Association, of which she was the chairperson at that time. Despite being busy attending to a very young baby, her daughter insisted on booking the ticket with her mobile phone. That circumstance may have contributed to the error that occurred, which was not realised at the time.

Julie got to the central station in Glasgow on her way out and proceeded to the ticket office to print out her ticket for the journey, and for the first time, she accepted a receipt for the transaction, which she promptly put in her handbag. Usually, she says 'no' to receipts when offered to her. A higher power was looking after her that day when one considers what transpired later on the journey. It was about 15 minutes into the journey that the ticket officer came to check her ticket, which she happily handed over to her. She took one look at it, and without any explanation, the lady walked off with the ticket while Julie was left wondering what had gone amiss. She had gone for back-up as she returned with another male colleague, so now, she had two officials on her case.

Julie's ticket had an earlier date than this travel date, as if the ticket had been used before, which would be fraudulent. Her daughter had mistakenly put the same date for both legs of the journey when purchasing the ticket online, which explains why Julie had gone to the 'wrong' seat number on arrival, and was promptly told by the occupant that the seat was rightfully his for that journey. She was quite confused and embarrassed but could not figure out what was wrong until the officials approached her. Julie told them that it was a case of the 'wrong' date and that she had just collected the ticket from the ticket office at the station. Then the officer asked her very loudly,

'Have you got a receipt for the transaction?' to which she loudly replied,

'Yes! I have just collected the ticket and receipt and entered the train 15 minutes ago.'

The receipt showed the time of collection, so it could not have been any fraud intended, but a genuine mistake had occurred. The conversation between Julie and the officers was very loud, benefitting the eavesdroppers pretending not to be interested in the saga going on around them. Who would not be curious to know how the whole drama played out?

Julie had no choice but to buy another return ticket, but she left the listeners without doubt about the mistake. Julie felt good that she could hold her head up but always wondered how it would have ended if she had not collected the receipt for the transaction that morning just before she got on the train. How would she have proven there and then that there was no fraud intended, that the ticket had not been used on a previous journey, and that the wrong date was booked? Even though she had to buy another one-way ticket for that journey, Julie whispered a silent prayer of thanks to God for watching over her actions that day and for the possession of plastic cards to solve money problems. Transport police could have got involved.

A lot of damage could have been done to her reputation because she might have had to answer the question for some visa application: 'Have you ever been arrested by the police, rightly or wrongly?'

That would have been very inconvenient indeed. Since that experience, Julie never leaves a shop without her receipt, no matter how small the amount is. Sometimes she gets weird looks when cashiers ask if she wants the receipt, and her answer is always, 'Yes, please,' even for 20p!

The lesson is never to judge someone when you do not know their motivation. Please do not assume that, because they are Black or for whatever reason, a crime has been committed when there might be a simple, innocent explanation, as in this case.

Julie finally settled down to begin her journey. Sitting on the train on that cold autumn day, Julie was as usual deep in thought about life. 'When will I ever start that book I have been planning to write?'; she pondered to herself over her many titles and many new starts, and she felt the plot in a maze. Julie uses motivational talk to pluck herself up when she gets in this self-deprecating mood. She tells herself that, once a baby is born, he or she starts a new life with a clean slate on this planet we call earth. And if the baby had not crawled or stood, he would not have taken that first step. Oh yes, and if he had not stumbled and fallen several times, he would not have appreciated the considerable accomplishment of walking and even running. Julie mused at her silly analysis of ordinary human reality.

Motivational reasoning is an exercise of the mind that Julie engages in as a stimulus to start her day or to take a step in any direction, be it to go for a walk, dress up for a party or especially something as serious as starting a new business. This last option would undoubtedly give even the bravest man a lot to ponder about, she sighs. This excuse settles that weakness once and for all for now.

Julie felt that time was running out for her dream to write a book. There were notes and reminders on every available notepad or piece of paper around her. Even her diary had scribbles of flashes of ideas and moments of inspiration. Julie reflected on how long the journey to this point had been. Julie was already an over-65-year-old African woman typical of her colonial generation. She was born in Nigeria into a Catholic family and was one of twelve children, so she was used to lots of drama. Julie was known to her family as the ultimate extrovert and drama queen. Her husband had recently passed after battling cancer for some time.

She has been on her own since being widowed and carrying out her parental duties as best as possible. Before then, she was a happily married woman who became a full-time housewife after moving to the UK from Nigeria. The move was not an easy transition for someone used to working at a corporate level, a house full of relatives, and house help. She had had to adjust and adapt very quickly to her new life in the UK. She had five children. In Nigeria, having a large family was considered a significant achievement by both sides of the family in her time and she was looked upon with respect in the community, especially when she finally succeeded in producing a male child! In the UK, however, it became apparent that five children were a large family.

Julie was the daughter of teachers from Southern Nigeria. Much was expected of her and her siblings regarding academic achievement and success. She was one of the early generations of women to go to a higher institution of learning in the part of the country where she was born. She worked as a civil servant in the Education department, as a teacher, and as a school inspector before relocating to Northern Ireland, United Kingdom, in the early 1980s to join her husband. After some time, they returned to Africa before returning to the UK, but this time to Scotland in 1996. This journey had its ups and downs. As for Julie, this immediately signified the loss of her career as a civil servant.

Even though she decided to study a postgraduate course in Education, her husband's itinerant life never allowed her to settle down in one place for long. He had worked in Northern Ireland, Wales, and England, and Julie delivered children in all three countries. Her husband also worked in Saudi Arabia for some years while the family lived in Nigeria. It felt as if they were always on the move, so much so that it was difficult to put down roots until his last ten years, which were spent in Scotland when her husband got a permanent consultant post on the island of Lewis. These past lives played out in Julie's mind as she sat on the train.

An announcement was made that the next train stop was Croy, which jolted Julie out of her reverie. She seemed to have woken up from a deep sleep and suddenly returned to reality and her environment. She looked out of the window and saw houses flying past and the train grinding slowly to a halt. It was a very small brown station house with double glass doors around a rectangular glasshouse. About ten passengers were waiting on the platform to enter the train while fewer people hopped out of the train. There was an obviously drunken man with a whisky bottle in hand who had the presence of mind to drop the empty bottle in the bin just before he climbed onto the train. 'Maybe, he is not as drunk as he looks,' Julie thought. He reminded her of the dishevelled detective Columbo in the eponymous US drama series, who always looks disorientated before coming out with his signature phrase, '… just one more thing …'.

Then she saw a passenger who was too slow entering the train have his head jammed between the doors, which quickly re-opened. 'That must have hurt.' Julie wondered if he was okay and whether he would sue the train operators. One could see the car parks around the little station from the train window. Julie cast her eyes beyond the cars and tried to look into the distance to get a feel of the village from the train, but all she could see were a couple of modern blocks of flats, not the village. The station car park was 100 yards away, and some passengers could be seen running straight from their cars, around the station house and into the train. She then heard the public announcement, 'Mind the gap, mind the gap', as the passengers stepped in and out of the train, and then, the train was off again.

Once again, Julie's thoughts returned to why she had to make this journey today. Her daughter was planning a wedding and insisted she come to help choose the wedding cake and dress. Conversation with Ade invariably ends up in an argument, no matter how the discussion is approached. Julie felt Ada could argue with a saint. Ada was a troublemaker in her mind, and hanging up the phone on her had become a sad habit of escaping escalating arguments. Her calls always left her feeling drained and angry afterwards. Their conversation always goes, 'Yea, anytime I ask you for a favour, you always have an excuse ...'

'Hold on! I can't just jump on a train. I live in Glasgow. I, I, I ...' Julie replies, stammering to answer.

These encounters were infuriating as Ada lives down south in Stockton-on-Tees.

Julie brought herself back to the present and the reason for this journey. Who could ever forget the fiasco of the last wedding cake for her other daughter? The cake almost toppled over as it was tilting to the side and hanging precariously on three cake stands that could hardly hold the weight of the top layer. Julie looked out of the window and saw a glistening train snaking thunderously past, going in the opposite direction. It did not stop at this station. Julie felt that it was surreal that we become so used to our environment that we forget that it was all so strange at the beginning. When she first arrived in the UK, she had never been on a train. Back in Nigeria, there were some rusty, ancient 'goods' trains she had seen on television, hurtling down creaky, worn-out colonial train tracks between some areas of the west and the north of the country. Standing passengers could be seen hanging out of every nook and corner of the train, holding onto whatever was available.

In contrast, the trains in the UK are passenger trains, which are luxurious and on time, most of the time. 'Time' is another big difference that Julie could consider between the UK and Nigeria. In Nigeria, we have 'African time' for everything. It is not surprising to receive an invitation card for 1.00 p.m. when the event kicks off at 4.00 p.m. The only exceptions are the orthodox churches trying their best to enforce timekeeping. Priests have been known to storm out of the church and lock themselves in the parish house until begged to come out to perform the wedding ceremony. Now, try to imagine the look of an angry priest conducting a wedding service! Orthodox priests are few and overworked, and people do not realise that they do not own the priest's time. They do not see that their attitude to timekeeping affects both their and the priest's spiritual and mental well-being.

Julie is not one to be very observant; her education did not prepare her for that. Still, she did notice that the weather had changed from cold and dry to rainy in two stops, reminding Julie of the typical British weather when four seasons can happen in one day. It was a coldish autumn day, and the landscape was dreary, damp and grey, with trees presenting their skeletal branches. On the farmlands could be seen rows and rows of brownish rolled hay. She looked beyond the fields to the undulating hills and coastline in the distance, partially covered by the morning dew. The river was still blue as it meandered along the coast. Julie glanced back into her carriage to watch passengers get on and off at Middlesbrough.

An elderly lady in a red coat stepped onto the train, and after a quick glance to the left and right, she decided to come into Julie's carriage on the right, walking past the toilet first. Julie always sits near the door, or rather, near the toilets, to be precise, as she seems to need to visit the toilet frequently. She suffers from a bit of 'just in case' incontinence. The lady made her way to the empty seat next to Julie, which was a pleasant surprise as there was another empty seat across the aisle. She usually benefits from two seats to herself, even when the carriage is full. Some passengers would leave the carriage to seek another seat elsewhere rather than sit next to an African woman. Overt racism has improved over the years, but having company was still a pleasant surprise.

Instinctively, Julie tried to make herself smaller to avoid touching the passenger sitting next to her. At some point, she became so stiff that she almost developed a cramp in her thighs, and she started shifting around awkwardly, trying to keep a polite distance and not touch the other passenger. She remembers accidentally touching a lady once and how she deliberately and pointedly brushed her side down and shifted ridiculously far away towards the aisle. However, Julie had breathed a sigh of relief because she could then relax and breathe. She had not realised that she had been sitting with stiffened shoulders, all in an attempt to reduce the breadth of her broad shoulders. It was unthinkable to relax and touch or rest your shoulder on a stranger as that would be very rude and inappropriate, so Julie always tried to be alert to proper deportment. She looked across the aisle at the man sitting in the adjacent seat. You would think he had bought two seats, judging by how he spread his legs wide, squashing the lady by the window into the side of the train.

Julie is usually a chatterbox, but today she was minding her own business as her children have advised her. Staring ahead with her head on the headrest, Julie was closing her eyes when she heard the lady in the red coat talking to her.

'So, where do you come from?' she asked.

Julie replied, 'I'm originally from Nigeria, but I live in Glasgow now.'

The lady then asked, 'So why did you leave your country and come to this country?'

Her tone was not friendly, so Julie quickly realised that this would not be a friendly conversation; it was an inquisition, so she pretended not to hear the question and leaned back on the headrest.

The lady asked her next question. 'So, what are you doing here?'

Julie lifted her head and looked the lady in the eye, and asked, 'Do you mean right now, on this train? I am doing what everyone else is doing, travelling on a train to visit family or on holiday or for business. What else is there to do?'

Julie promptly rested her head back and turned her face to the window as the tannoy announced Stockton-on-Tees as the next stop. This questioning was common, 'a life in the day of Julie'. Scrambling to her feet, Julie reached up to get her bag from the overhead luggage compartment and exited the train. As she pulled her suitcase along the platform hurrying towards the north exit, she knew she had reached her destination today, but the journey would continue tomorrow.

Chapter 3

ADVENTURES AND MISADVENTURES

A visit to the village

Julie was an inquisitive and restless child, always asking to go away on holidays to aunties, uncles, and Grandma, unlike some of her siblings who were not fussed about being stuck at home all summer holidays. It was the tradition in Julie's tribe and most others to allow one's children to go away from the family to uncles, aunties, and grandparents on school holidays and to receive visiting children too. People had huge families, so it was not always possible for everyone to go away at the same time. It was not part of the tradition for whole families to visit another family or go away to a hotel. About eight to twelve persons were in monogamous homes in the

1960s. A polygamous home could have two to four wives and as many as twenty children in one household at any time. It is therefore not difficult to understand how a 'family' holiday was impossible. It is only quite recently, in the past 40 years, that modern families with fewer children have started to go away together on holiday.

In polygamous homes, there would be competition amongst the wives whose children had willing aunties, uncles, and grandparents to visit. It was a good experience for the children to go away from home to another safe environment and explore other things they did not have in their own environment. An example is Julie and her siblings being allowed to go with Cousin Mabel to visit her family during the holiday. Mabel came from the village and grew up in Julie's family home in Benin City, just like Julie's father, who had come from a rural area to the city to live with relatives when he was a teenager. He had come from the village to live with an uncle in the city to further his education.

Mabel's father was a subsistence farmer with some extra produce left for the markets on market days. Her mother was also a farmer and a trader who sold refined farm produce like 'garri' (grains made from cassava) and vegetables in the market. They had their own modest house in the village made with cement blocks and a zinc roof, with outside bathrooms and toilets. The compound was impeccably swept and neat. Julie and her siblings were allowed to visit the village with Mabel during the school holidays. They always came back to the city with tales of the unexpected about village life, and they always learnt new skills like fishing, basket making and mat weaving, or how to make 'garri' from cassava or 'akamu' (custard) from corn. Julie's parents were teachers and relished these learning opportunities and the passing on of these skills on their return.

The difference between the rural areas of Nigeria and the towns and cities is very stark. Rural areas usually lack modern facilities and infrastructure like electricity and tarred roads. The poorest of houses could be built with mud and thatch, while others were built with blocks, zinc roofs, and basic comforts. Most people in rural areas depend on subsistence farming for their livelihood. Excess produce is usually taken to the market to sell on market days. The rural areas do not have extra-curricular activities, like sporting facilities, zoos, cinemas or high-end restaurants. The schools are usually in a state of disrepair. In some instances, children walked quite long distances to get to school.

On the other hand, the towns and cities were very cosmopolitan, with all the infrastructure found in cities: traffic lights, traffic jams, primary and secondary schools and higher institutions, hospitals, and health centres, as well as modern buildings and modern infrastructure. Having electricity in the city does not guarantee constant light; lack of infrastructure maintenance is the norm, such that nothing works as it should. Many people get by with owning their generators and sinking a borehole for their water. This situation benefits businessmen and women and the corrupt politicians who sell generators, so they do not allow things to change for the better. Things are, at best, chaotic and lacking in planning by the government departments. The government contracted the electricity out to private enterprises, and since then, the situation has worsened for everyone. One is lucky to get eight hours of light in a whole day. Some rural areas are connected to electricity.

When visiting relatives in the village, it was a regular occurrence that a child would cry that he or she wanted to go home with Aunty or Uncle, often goaded on by their mothers from behind. In Mabel's case, however, Julie's dad had asked to take her with him to the city so that she could further her education beyond primary school. Julie's dad was an educationist who 'rescued' many children by bringing them into his home and training them to be the best they could be. It was the norm in those days for the leaders in the community to mentor less privileged children by taking them under their wing. He produced teachers, nurses, and executives like Mabel, who later retired as the personnel manager of a large corporation.

The day Julie's father visited his cousin in the village just 30 minutes from the city, he noticed an adolescent girl sitting around doing 'nothing' on the way to his village farm just ten minutes away. Her dad said she had finished primary school and was helping her mother with farming. Dad knew the next logical thing would be a baby and poverty for her, like other young women in the village. He was an educator and father of eleven girls and one boy, who passionately believed in women's education. He brought her home with him.

Julie's mum was used to children being dumped on her by relatives. Some simply turned up on the doorstep with their children and with all their worldly possessions wrapped in a cloth cupped under their armpit. Most of the children were taken in and educated, but some could not stay, as they could not tolerate the discipline expected of them. As one cousin said, the house was a 'prison'; one was not allowed to enter any neighbouring house or bring in undesirable friends. Later in life, he wished he had stayed to be educated and get off the streets. That would certainly have stood him in better stead than he is now, a wheelbarrow loader in the market, taking shoppers' goods to their cars!

Julie's dad was a pioneer and a visionary when it came to the education of girls. He was a teacher first and foremost, then a headmaster, a churchwarden and later an elected member of parliament who had a passion for helping others and fighting for social justice and the common good. All his eleven daughters, one son and adopted children ended up with multiple qualifications, professional and technical, and had jobs in all sectors of the economy and are decent members of society.

Julie's parents knew the value of exposing their children to other experiences to learn how others lived and appreciate their opportunities. They always shared in the excitement when the children came back with stories of their exploits. The first thing her parents made her do was to write a story of 'what you did during your school holidays'. Julie's mum was a primary school teacher too. She noticed that anytime they returned from holiday, there was always a glow and excitement about them. They never wanted to come back home from holidays in the countryside, because there they could run wild and enjoy the fresh air, and the holiday was never more than a week, so there was no time to get fed up with it. There was also an atmosphere of tranquillity, and sweet fresh fruits ripened on the trees: mangoes, pears, pineapples, sour sops, sugarcane, avocados, bananas, etc. – they had them all. There was even fresh fish from the rivers then. However, there was no electricity, televisions, or fancy goods as one found in the cities.

Eventually, though, electricity got to some villages even if it was not regular. Even in 2022, the electricity supply is very sporadic and unreliable in big cities. People are surviving by supplementing with generators which is a significant blight on the economy. The cost of powering the generators comes at a high cost to businesses.

The excitement and build-up to the holiday always made the holiday worthwhile. Hosts spent time and resources entertaining children and giving them memorable experiences. Julie's parents wanted their children to experience other cultures, and they were also wary of them overstaying their welcome. The only exception to this one-week rule was her maternal grandparents, who lived in the city. There, Julie and her siblings could spend unlimited time on holiday unless they fell ill, and then Mum insisted on them returning home for treatment.

Visiting the rural area was always a positive experience so long as one did not foolishly run into a forest without an experienced person and step on a snake's head! There were snakes in town bushes and footpaths too. It's funny that country children looked upon town children with admiration and envy for the nice clothes and shoes on their feet. Town children envied the village kids in their serene environment, full of peace, with no hooting noise from cars, fresh fruits, running wild and playing outside all day, no gates, storytelling under the moonlight, and no studying or going to church for catechism. When away from home, one is treated like royalty and gets away with many pranks that could not happen at home.

Life at home was regimented, like a boarding school during the holidays. Everyone had morning duties, such as sweeping the rooms with a broom, washing clothes, or assisting with cooking. There were no blenders then; scotch bonnet peppers, onions and tomatoes were ground on smooth grinding stones. One can only imagine the havoc it used to do to the nostrils and the pain in one's hands from the pepper for hours. Clothes were hand-washed in a basin. Then, there was time for studying or just reading a novel, and there was no point pretending to read because you would be caught out if you did not. How would you write a summary of the story later? Mum always insisted on a written summary. That was the 'peril' of being the children of zealous teachers!

There was time for play in the front or back of the house, but children from her mum's house were not allowed to step outside the boundaries of their house into someone else's compound. After Julie grew up, she understood her mother's reasons for being so strict. Being a mother of ten daughters, she was extra vigilant in safeguarding her children against predatory men. On several occasions, one heard stories of kids having been raped by some random tenants in some of the overcrowded houses on the street. Sometimes, one heard the commotion and saw the gatherings of onlookers, especially when police officers arrived to investigate the case. Her mum was, therefore, as careful as possible, especially when they were younger and always gave rigorous instructions to anyone to whom she released her children. In any case, they knew her expectations and were eager not to fail in their duty.

A visit to Asaba

When Julie was ten years old, she visited her uncle Patrick and his wife in Asaba, a town in Mid-Western Nigeria, now in Delta State, while he was working there as a theatre nurse in the Government General Hospital. Asaba was about an hour's drive from Benin City. Uncle and Aunty had no children then, so nieces and nephews were always welcome to visit during the holidays. The compound was a small estate that housed about twenty families in small apartments like one or two-bedroom twin bungalows or terraces built as an L-shape, which belonged to the council and came with the job. Julie was instructed to play in front of the bungalow in the children's communal area, and never enter any apartment, even though occupants were government workers. It was school holiday time, so many children were in the compound, as well as the children from some neighbouring compounds. All the children played together while the stay-at-home mums conspicuously kept an eye on them.

On one particularly hot day, her uncle had gone to work. Her unemployed aunt then decided to go to the market for groceries and left her to play with the other kids after repeated warnings not to venture away from the compound. She left Julie in the care of some women who were sitting on little stools on the veranda, holding their babies. All the women sat on stools near their front doors and were chatting with each other across the doors, and Julie remembers that she was left to no one in particular. It was just a general appeal to all the women to look out for the newbie and that her aunt would be back soon. Before long, one of the kids suggested a trip to the nearby river. All the children agreed to do it, and Julie also went along after some hesitation. She glanced at the veranda, but by this time, the women watching them were nowhere to be seen; they had gone inside their flats.

Julie felt free to explore with the other kids as no one was there to stop her. As they got there, the kids started jumping into the river and swimming up and down like pros, so Julie thought it looked easy and jumped into the river. Of course, this city girl knew nothing about swimming and immediately started to swallow water and drown, and the kids did not notice. It was divine intervention that there happened to be a woman on the riverbank washing her clothes who took notice of the unfamiliar face whose clothes and shoes stood out when she glanced up at their arrival. She was the one that raised the alarm and jumped into the river to save Julie from drowning. It took a while for Julie to stop spluttering water from her mouth and nostrils and be able to sit up and breathe. Julie almost caused a breakdown in her uncle and aunt's marriage as Aunty was blamed for 'allowing' it to happen. What would he have told his older brother and his wife? Julie can still hear the loud argument and fighting into the night after the incident.

A cobra at Christmas time

This story reminds Julie of other near-death incidents in which she had been directly involved. As the African adage goes, she was a 'tortoise that's never-ending in stories'. Most African tales were about the exploits of the tortoise and the hare, 'Cinderella and the wicked stepmother', and brothers and sisters taken away to a distant land, who disappeared on the way to farms, and were then taken across the big river by foreigners. Some of the tales turned out to be oral history, even if we did not know that at the time – for example, the Trans-Atlantic slave trade.

One hot Christmas Day, when Julie was about 10 years old, she encountered a cobra, a deadly snake. Usually, they went to the zoo in Benin to see wild animals but never expected to see a huge snake in the grass so close to her on the street in a big city. Christmas Day in Southern Nigeria was like no other day. It was a day of celebration of the birth of Jesus for those who were Christians. There was the usual build-up to the day with children getting their only new clothes of the year made. Julie's mum used to take them to the 'London-trained tailor', as she advertised herself on the signboard. Mum became her customer and her friend. Mum could never get over the fact that the tailor's husband had operated on a dog. He was a veterinary surgeon, but it was a strange story in Benin at that time. Julie remembers Mum saying, 'White people are very funny and strange. How can you operate on a dog, and it survives?'

Operating on a dog was a very alien concept to her as she had never heard of it. It had not entered Julie's mother's mind that perhaps, in Ogba Zoo, operations were carried out on animals. Some people working with the animals were expatriate workers or foreigners. Children used to visit the zoo to see all the exotic animals from the wild, like lions, zebras, elephants, snakes, etc., which they had read about in books. It was a huge zoo occupying a large area where the animals were presented in their natural habitat.

Contrary to the belief of some friends in the UK, no wild animals were roaming the streets of towns and cities in Africa, not even in village settings. Wild animals are found in the forest or the zoo. The husband of the tailor Julie and her family patronised was a veterinary surgeon at the zoo.

Whenever they visited the tailor, she had a selection of materials she stocked to make it easy for parents, especially when choosing materials for children's 'English' wear in Littlewoods or British Home Store catalogues. The tailor was very good at recreating posh-looking clothes for girls from those British catalogues like Littlewoods. Julie and her siblings always got two sets of clothes at Christmas: English wear and African print. The English wear was the outfit made with 'foreign' fabrics in the style of dresses in the UK shops and worn with a hat, bow, or ribbons in the hair. In contrast, the African wear was made of floral-patterned African prints and was always made in the traditional style of a blouse, skirt/wrapper, and a matching head tie. The young boys would wear a suit if they could afford it or a shirt and trousers, but Julie's only brother always wore a suit, so Mum made sure that it was big enough to wear for two years, even if it meant folding the sleeves and trousers in the first year! The only thing new for the boy was probably a new shirt, and for the African print, he always wore a 'buba' and 'sokoto' with a matching cap.

'Buba' and 'sokoto' are traditional two-piece outfits that men wear in Africa; it could be a three-piece outfit if the 'agbada' is added. The agbada is a big, wide, flowing regal piece worn on top of buba and sokoto. On Christmas Day, it was the tradition in Julie's home to wear the English outfit to church and to keep it on for the rest of the day until after all the visitors had stopped coming. Christmas Days used to be very exciting days as the children could not wait to show off their new clothes. Nobody wanted to enter the car to go to church, unlike regular Sundays when some cried to get in the car. The car could not take everyone anyway, and only the youngest children got in, but on Christmas Day, they begged to walk to the church. They wanted everyone to see them in their new English outfits.

The build-up to Christmas Day was always exciting for everybody. The tempo of activities increased with people shopping as if there was no tomorrow or the market would run out of goods, just like Christmas shopping in the UK, all for one day, Christmas Day. The preparation would start weeks before with materials given to the tailor, for one would not find a tailor to accept the clothes at the last minute because tailors would be overwhelmed. One was always advised to make clothes early, but it never worked out that way. The 'poor' tailors have been known to sew all night into Christmas morning and through to New Year, as this was their busiest time to make money. Apart from the clothes to be worn, attention was paid to girls' hair. The boys just went to the barbers to get their hair cut, while girls' hairstyles involved braiding, plaiting, combing into afro style or straightening with hot comb.

Julie and some of her siblings were in a Catholic boarding school where hair braiding and plaiting were not allowed because of the length of time it took to look after the hair. They had to cut their hair short but stylish, so long as it was easy to keep clean and tidy, apart from in the final year when students could plait their hair. The present generation has discarded this rule, but there are still rules about acceptable hairstyles. In Julie's time, the holiday was a time to plait the hair and make it long so that, on party days, the hair could be loosened and combed into a big afro hairstyle. Julie's mum dressed the hair with a hair band like a bandana, or she just tied a ribbon around the hair into a round bun on top of the head.

As they grew older, Julie noticed that the fashion changed for the older ones who wanted to straighten their hair with a hot iron comb. The hot iron was placed on hot coal and used to comb out the oiled hair in sections. Sometimes the hot oil from the hair dropped on the neck, or the hot comb burnt the neck or top of the ear in incompetent hands – all this suffering in the name of fashion. Julie's mum allowed some liberties at Christmas, after which the hair was cut low, and the hot-pressed hair was washed and back to its natural state before school began again. Julie and her classmates were allowed to plait their hair in the final year of secondary school, mostly corn rows in different styles. Hair extensions were not permitted, only natural hair. She supposed that that was preparation for leaving school and going out into the bigger world.

The Irish nun who was the principal brought in women from the community on some Saturdays and allowed them to use the school hall to plait their hair for some payment. She did not want any pressure on any student who had the skill to do it as that would distract them from their studies, especially the junior students who were not allowed to plait hair for seniors. It was a serious offence that could lead to expulsion from school if any senior bullied a junior to plait her hair, so it was a blanket ban.

Apart from shopping, tailors, and hairdressing, travellers could be seen in queues for 'luxurious buses' (coaches) mostly heading towards the east, with passengers trying to get to their home towns and villages for Christmas. Julie's family home was near the main road that connected the east to the west, and the biggest market in the city was along the main road, just at the end of her street. At that time of the year, everywhere in the vicinity felt like part of the market because of hawkers and makeshift seasonal kiosks/stalls that sold anything from cartons of cabin biscuits to live chickens. Hawkers ran alongside the buses, selling their goods to the passengers. Julie had a cousin who said she could sell 50 boxes of cabin biscuits to travellers daily during the festive period.

While all the selling and buying was happening, there were also the musicians and street entertainers doing their own thing. They depended on people's festive generosity for donations. The most iconic entertainers were the masquerades, all dressed in heavy costumes made of layers of red fabric and raffia. Faces were painted with white chalk or charcoal, heads covered, and three-quarters of their faces were covered apart from the eyes. They were very good at tumbling and somersaulting. When Julie was young, she believed that the masquerades had magical and spiritual powers, so the kids used to run in to hide until their parents coerced them to come out and watch the display. There were one or two masquerades and their accompanying group of followers played the drums and gongs and some traditional instruments made of wood and bamboo performed to entertain the crowds.

Masquerades were only seen at festive times, including Christmas and traditional festivals on the town's calendar. Usually, the songs were all praise-singing and prayers for the occupants of the home, with the hope of getting money donated to them. If they sang and danced for too long without getting any money, the tune soon changed to subtle abuse, which the kids thought was hilarious at the time. The truth was that too many dance troupes were competing for the money; some came ill-prepared and underdressed but expecting quick money, or the homeowners ran out of change.

A lot of food was cooked in every home, with goat meat and chicken. The more live goats and chickens you had in your compound paraded for days before the day, the more affluent you were. Sometimes the animals were Christmas gifts from younger siblings to the head of the family or from children who had grown up and left home. Julie's father sometimes gifted some goats to the church or some other extended family, patriarch, or friend. These animals were usually slaughtered and skinned and prepared in the home by 'butchers', every family having someone who played that role, but in recent times, professionals have been hired to perform the tasks. There were arguments about what part of the cow the butcher was entitled to by tradition. They filled up a large bucket with all the best parts, using some outdated superstitious narrative to 'steal' the best parts of the cow. Customers have set aside tradition and refused to part with the best parts of their cow, especially after paying for the service. The fights were all part of the shenanigans surrounding the celebrations.

There was always an open fire made at the back of the house on big iron stoves or blocks arranged with firewood lit under a wide iron grid for roasting the whole goats and chickens before they were cut up and used to make stews or just spiced, boiled, and fried. The butcher put meat on sheets of clean zinc for scraping before washing, and they always found a suitable bench made of planks for cutting up the meat. This cooking usually took place from the evening of Christmas Eve up until the morning of Christmas Day. Everyone gathered around to watch and help out once the cooking got underway. Some paternal aunties and uncles from the village came over in the morning and stayed the whole day. Some young children in their Sunday best usually came as early as 7.30 a.m. to eat rice or pounded yam with soup or moi-moi (bean cake), meat, chin-chin (pastry snack) and drinks. The children also expected to leave with sweets and money, which they went home to share, almost like trick-or-treat, except it was for the hot food.

The children were always welcomed happily, for what was the point of cooking if no one turned up to eat it? There was always a buzz to have kids start coming relatively early in the day, and all dressed up. There were houses that nobody would go into, either because they did not have provisions, or were tenants, or single young people. Sometimes, food was exchanged by families who were old allies. Sometimes also, fresh meat was exchanged for cooked food, especially when a cow had been slaughtered.

Julie and her siblings were not allowed to go into random houses, only specially selected ones, and they were not allowed to eat at any house as some children did. One could see from the size of their stomachs that some children were struggling to swallow another mouthful. One felt guilty if the food was not offered, but now looking back on it, Julie wishes people had thought of take-away packs at the time. For some of those children, that was the best food they would have for months. Julie's mum did not allow her children to go about eating because she was a very proud woman who felt that her children were not disadvantaged, and the idea of her children eating from house to house did not sit well with her.

However, she could not resist the need to show off their Christmas clothes, as her children were always impeccably turned out. So, she allowed three or four of the younger children to walk in a group to visit their dad's sister and her cousin who lived nearby, but with very strict instructions not to eat food. She, therefore, made sure that they ate plenty of food before setting off on the short ten-minute round trip. This permission made the children very excited to join all the other children in their Christmas clothes, going from house to house; it gave them some freedom to be like their peers.

On one of those visits, Julie encountered a cobra on Christmas Day. The streets were paved with a very narrow strip of coal tar running through the middle; the rest of the sides were untarred, and the footpath along the street had knee-high grass on either side. Julie held on to her younger sister's hand as they walked along the path in pairs. As they went along excitedly, she suddenly heard the rustling of dry leaves on the ground and looked down to see a continuous movement and rustling leaves following them along in the grass. She was shocked to see the raised wide and flat head of a cobra trying to position itself for a strike. She was lucky that no car was coming because she did not think before running into the street, pulling the little one along while screaming to her two siblings in front to run for it.

The experience left them badly shaken, so they were still flustered when they got to their aunt's house. They narrated their experience and were told they were lucky because it was not unheard of for people to die of snake bites. Julie thought that happened only in the bush or forest, not along a busy footpath parallel to a busy tarred road. Aunty offered them food and tried to persuade them to eat, which they politely refused with the excuse that they were not hungry. That was when Julie's younger 5-year-old sister thought of what it was possible to have and stepped in and impatiently announced, 'We're not here to eat; just give us money, and we can go.'

Julie was so embarrassed that she wished the floor would open up and swallow her. Not everyone gave money; it was optional and not compulsory. The siblings are now in their sixties, and this story is still the stuff of legend.

More snakes

Julie's encounter with snakes did not end with that roadside experience with the cobra on Christmas Day. This next episode was the final straw that pushed her over the bar. Today, Julie has a phobia of snakes to the extent that a plastic snake can cause so much revulsion in her body that she becomes physically sick. This encounter happened on Mission Road in Benin City. As the name suggests, it was named by the colonial 'masters' long before Nigerian independence. It is the high street and the oldest main road in Benin, which happened to link her grandmother's house in the old part of town to her father's house in the newer part of town. Julie was on her way to her grandparents to visit her uncles, who were home on holiday from the university outside of their state, when she saw her uncle's friend as she walked along the pavement. He was driving a Volkswagen Passat car and pulled up beside her to offer her a lift down the road. He was a good friend of her Uncle Tony and well known to everyone in her grandma's house and known to Julie as a seasoned news broadcaster on the local radio.

The city was relatively safe in those days, especially in broad daylight and in public, especially if someone was not a stranger to you. Julie did not hesitate before jumping into the car. It was common practice to accept lifts from car owners in those days. When she was already seated, and he drove off, making small talk, he drew her attention to her surroundings inside the car. She still finds what she saw that day as incredible as the day it happened. The floor on the passenger side, the back seat, and the back seat floor were full of crawling snakes. She crunched her knees to her chin and started screaming to be let out of the car. Uncle Tony's friend tried to reassure her that they were harmless species, but she was having none of it. She was paralysed with fear and broke out in a sweat. Even when he stopped to let her out and leaned across to open the passenger

68

door, she was too frightened to lower her legs. She just kept screaming, which attracted the attention of curious passers-by who had stopped to watch what was happening.

Onlookers, now involved in the drama, looked as he lifted her from the car's passenger side, applauding with amusement. By the time he drove off, Julie had many sympathisers consoling and warning her of the dangers of accepting lifts. Julie later learnt from her uncle that he was also the zookeeper in the city's zoo. They had never got a chance to hold a conversation before she saw the snakes. Uncle Tony promised to admonish him for that silly prank. One could have had a heart attack, finding oneself inside a car full of snakes. It was a hard lesson learnt to be careful who to trust.

Thunder and lightning

Julie considers herself a fortunate person, having survived accidents and deadly situations. It was strange but true that it was on an errand from her mum to the same aunt they were visiting when they had the encounter with the cobra that Julie experienced what a danger thunderbolts were. Mum and Aunty belonged to the same social club, and Julie often ran errands between them. Sometimes it was simply to say, 'Sorry, I cannot come to the meeting today, due to ill health.'

There were no mobile phones then, and members were expected to send their apologies through another member if they could not attend a meeting. If no message was sent, they were fined, and Julie knew that money was tight, so her mum would always send her apology through her sister-in-law. That day, the errand was to deliver African print materials to Aunty Ameze and bring back the money. Aunty was to choose between two African print materials. Julie's mum was on the dress code committee for the annual dance event they were planning. Nigerians have a tradition of club members and families identifying themselves by 'aso-ebi' – simply a homogeneous group wearing the same identifying outfit for special occasions. In this case, it was for the annual charity dance of the club.

She was instructed several times not to lose the money but her mum, Margaret, was always one to be repetitive and sarcastic while giving instructions. It was a cloudy day, and Mum said, 'Run down to your aunty with these fabrics and run back before the rain starts. The sky is looking grey. Make sure you collect the money from her, and after that, play and play until you lose the money in the mud before coming home.'

She simply had to say, 'Please do not lose the money.' However, that would not be Julie's mum talking. The family were used to her funny ways of expressing herself, which might sometimes be sarcasm. Mum would never wake you up in the morning properly; instead, if you were running late for an appointment, she would stand near the door and keep saying, while making enough noise to wake you up! 'Keep on sleeping. Just keep on sleeping. I won't wake you up. Just keep on sleeping. Do not go for your appointment.'

Julie and her siblings still laugh about a catalogue of such instructions while growing up. While helping her daughter with child minding, she is famously known for telling her granddaughter, 'Turn the soup, turn it, turn it very well. Eat all the meat so that when your mum comes back, there will be nothing left for her to eat.'

Julie hurried out along the footpath, only stopping once to chat with her friend briefly as she hopped along. Within a few minutes, the sky became very dense, and it started to rumble loudly with lots of flashes of lightning. Suddenly, a lightning bolt touched down ferociously, directly in front of her. It was a blinding flash that hit the ground and went up again at incredible speed. She was about 12 years old, so she was old enough to realise that she had just narrowly missed death by thunder strike. It was an eerie experience, and she always shudders anytime she remembers the incident.

Date with a tanker

Recounting her near-death tales is Julie's favourite pastime. It reminds her of how lucky she is to still be alive. Some of those near-death experiences were unforgettable. Her encounter with a huge trailer is another example of why she is lucky to still be counted among the living. She always wonders if everyone else has experienced as many near-death incidents. Julie always reminds herself that God saved her on that particular day for a purpose. She was 22 years old, and soon after, she started a new job as an education officer at the state's Ministry of Education, and she had just learned to drive.

She was driving along the famous Mission Road that runs through the city's centre, from Kings Square in the north, to down south through the New Benin area. Halfway along this road is an intersection with another very long road going through Benin from the Lagos highway in the west all the way across the city to the east of the city on the way out to the Eastern part of the country. This road was perilous because most cars, lorries, coaches, tankers, and trailers were not local; they were driving through the city. It was before a bypass was built to circumvent the city and divert heavy traffic and huge vehicles away from the city centre.

Most of the drivers were very reckless and had no thought whatsoever for the safety of other road users or most locals going about their daily business. In fact, rumour has it that the drivers of the 'luxurious' buses (coaches) and tankers used to put a boulder on the accelerator to keep the vehicle on top speed non-stop. Julie was inclined to believe this after her near-death experience at the intersection. She was driving north from the south while the trailer was speeding from the west towards the east. One would expect every vehicle to slow down while approaching the intersection, but that did not happen. Julie had tentatively entered the middle before realising that the trailer was at top speed and would not slow down, and it was too late to retreat. She made it through by a whisker. She could have been crushed to a pulp, and the tanker or trailer would not even stop until they were apprehended far away in another city. The driver's excuse was always that they were escaping from mob justice.

The incident was so traumatising that Julie could not drive for more than 15 minutes afterwards, as she had parked the car by the roadside to recover from the shock. She leaned against the car, shaking, with her hands folded across her chest and her head bowed in thanksgiving. As usual in such situations, an excited crowd gathered to congratulate her on her narrow escape. Some who had witnessed the incident stopped their cars to join the gathering crowd. They said, 'This happens every day. Heavy vehicles should be banned from going through the city.'

They went on to relate horror stories of fatalities from previous accidents at the crossroad. No one was sure who owned the right of way as many drivers were uneducated and did not understand or respect any traffic rules. They wake up, get in the car and steer. Once the car is moving, they call that driving. However, they do not know road signs and traffic rules and do not understand that they are responsible for other people's lives, as a moving vehicle can be a lethal weapon.

Tales of armed robbers

Julie wondered, 'How many people have had the "privilege" of a shoot-out with robbers in their own home and survived?' Julie did! It happened to her when she - was living in Benin City, Nigeria, in the 1980s. Julie and her family had returned to Nigeria for some years while her husband went out to work in Saudi Arabia. During that period, her mother gave Julie her late father's old hunting Dane gun to take to the police station for safekeeping. But Julie's husband Isaac decided to register it in his name and keep it. Occasionally, they would hear unusual noises in the compound in the dead of night, so on one such occasion at 3.00 a.m. Isaac shot the gun into the air from an upstairs window to warn the thieves he owned a gun. Julie also had a car stolen from her at gunpoint before the security guard could open the gate for her to drive in.

It was her sister's traditional wedding day, so she took a separate car to get there early to help with the preparations, arranging all the bride's outfits and ensuring that all service providers had brought their goods. There were no event planners in those days. The family planned everything by themselves, assigning people chores according to their skills. For anyone unfamiliar with Nigerian weddings, it is usually a double wedding: the traditional wedding and the church wedding for those who are Christians. Nowadays, one can even say there are three weddings because the registry marriage is compulsory for anyone who wants to be legally married; the marriage certificate given in the church is the certificate from the registry.

The registry affair used to be just the couple's administrative forms which were then sent to the church unless the couple had no intention of having a church wedding. In that case, the couple would celebrate with all their family in their wedding outfits and have a reception, according to everyone's pocket and taste. The traditional ceremonies are the most important for the families, so the elders do not even bother attending the church wedding. The traditional wedding used to be a small affair if one was planning a church wedding and reception. Over the decades, this has become a big party with canopies, decorations, cake, live bands, professional caterers, and the bride changing into many glitzy expensive outfits. It sometimes looks like a carnival with aunties from both sides competing with their aso-ebi outfits and head ties. It is usually a very colourful event with plenty of food and dancing into the night.

Nigerians love parties and will use any excuse to have one, as weekend parties start on Friday evenings and go on until Monday mornings. Julie had a great time at the wedding party, but she oversaw the young girls assigned to collect the money being 'sprayed' on the couple as they danced. This money is usually scattered on the floor and requires young people to pick it up and hand it over to Aunty to hold. The money collected at weddings usually goes a long way to paying off the wedding bills. Some couples and parents may owe providers of services and promise to pay off all their debts after collecting donations, so keeping an eye on the money was a serious job. This job did not stop Julie from dancing throughout, as she had to be on the floor whenever the married couple were up dancing. Even when they were sitting down, people would still walk up to 'spray' them with money or stuff an envelope into their hands which was promptly handed over to Julie. The job of 'holding money' was honourable because it meant you were trusted.

She offered to drop off her uncle and his wife on the way home, as they lived somewhere along her route. When she got home at about 8.00 p.m., she beeped her horn and sat back, waiting patiently for the 'gateman' (security man) to open the gate. Sometimes he patrolled the compound and could be at the back of the house when someone was at the gate. One just had to bleep the horn and wait, as it was impossible to open the gate from the outside. Before Julie could register what was happening around her, she felt her driver's door yanked open from under her hand, which was resting on the open window with the elbow pointing outside. She looked up and locked eyes with this young man who was about 25 years old. He had dreadlocks and bloodshot eyes and was sneering at her. He also had a strong smell of herbs and alcohol that filled the air. He wore dark clothes with a bandana on his head. Julie supposed he had to prepare himself for his job of invading other people's space by being 'high' to give him courage and power.

She looked towards the passenger's side and saw another young man leaning into the car through the window. He also looked in his twenties but had a very baby face, though not as vicious as the one on the driver's side. Then she heard the one on the driver's side speaking to her. He was dishing out commands like an army captain, except that he added some respect. 'Madam, come out, hands in the air.' Julie froze on the spot with fear and the realisation that these were armed carjackers. She remained seated, with hands shaking violently. He repeated his command, this time with more emphasis on every word in a very theatrical and 'respectful' way: 'M-a-d-a-m, come o-u-t!'

Holding the door open, he bent towards her and waved her out with both hands, making a mockingly dramatic bow as he ushered her out of the car. Julie had to come out of the car with her hands in the air, leaving all her possessions behind. The men got in the car, reversed, and drove off with her big holdall bag containing all her jewellery, cosmetics, wedding clothes and shoes, and her handbag in which were the house keys. When attending family weddings, it was customary for everyone to bring all their nice jewellery so that everyone could help choose the best for the bride. Julie thanked God that, at the last minute, she had decided to drop the bag of money collected with her mother, who had locked it in her trunk box and put the key in her bra while complaining that too many relatives were entering her room. The robbers must have followed her from the party because she had collected the money in a big bag. It was an open-air party under huge canopies, and onlookers usually stood around to watch, even when they were not part of the party.

As Julie waited for the gate to open, her husband was inside the house, clueless about the robbery going on outside his gate. She worried that her husband had heard the beep of her car horn and was praying that he did not come out to help or call the security guard. Robbers could be very nervous and violent when men were involved and were more likely to use their weapons when they saw a man. There were no mobile phones then, but nowadays, security guards are alerted by phone as one approaches the gate so that the gate flies open, and there is no need to beep the horn. The mobile phone has substantially reduced car jackings at the gate but does not stop the more daring ones who drive straight in with you in another car, pull the driver out, jump in and drive off in seconds! So, the by-word is vigilance. One must make sure that no car is following at close proximity as one approaches the gate. Yes, it was mentally exhausting, but it became a habit. In case you were wondering what happened to Julie's car, it was found in a rural community near the highway three days later. According to police reports, the car had been used for highway robbery, terrorising travellers and robbing them of their goods for three days.

Julie's car was found with the four doors wide open, and five passports (without visas) belonging to one family were inside. The owners of the passports may have had visa appointments in Lagos that day. There was a gasoline-filled container in the boot, and many torn documents belonging to victims were strewn everywhere in the car. Surprisingly, there was no physical damage to the car. The police declared the car an 'exhibit' which they had to process at police headquarters. The family had to pay all the bills for towing the car to the police headquarters. It was then released to them the next day. It was a frantic time because if the car was left in the vast police car park, it could lose its engine before being retrieved. That would have been another 'wahala' (palaver).

Robbers can be a menace in Nigeria. They sometimes terrorise rough neighbourhoods, sometimes going from house to house. The only people safe from robbers are those with the resources to build very high walls, deploy security cameras and employ armed security guards and security operatives who travel with them outside the home. Not all robbers are violent; some are just petty crooks, but none can be trusted not to resort to violence if they are cornered or challenged. They use many ruses to strike a targeted person. For instance, a man once drove to a home and asked for the 'madam' of the house to tell her that her son's school had sent him to inform her that her son was ill. Her son was in a Jesuit boarding school, and there were no reliable land lines and no mobile phones at that time, so it would not be unusual to send someone to deliver a message to a family.

Naturally, the woman panicked, ran inside to get her car keys and ordered the lone security man to open the gate, only to get to the gate and be stopped by a gang of robbers pointing a gun at her. The security guard was held at gun point while the gang members emptied the house into the car, took all the money and jewellery they could find and drove off with everything. They were lucky that no one got hurt. That story was just a ruse to get the gate open and hold the occupants of the home at gun point. Everyone was on high alert for all sorts of tricks, so robbers became less successful at using them.

The one sure opportunity to expose oneself to robbers was having workmen come to the house to fix things. Not all workmen are culpable; the majority are honest, hardworking people and decent members of society. The problems are the minority of workmen who come into a home and see it as an opportunity to survey the layout to return later to steal – not that one would be able to prove it most of the time.

In Nigeria, there is a tradition of encouraging young men who have dropped out of school or finished primary school to go for apprenticeships. Some of these apprentices could also hold a Secondary School Leaving Certificate. These apprenticeships are usually in vocational careers like plumbing, electrical work, car repairs and maintenance, or carpentry. Most of the time, the apprentices are diligent in learning the trade, but some congregate in these places to plan mischief. One such gang went on a highway robbery rampage and ended up at the door of one of their victims, who recognised the 'captain' when he needed a carpenter to fix his leaking roof.

A month before then, Isaac had brought in a consignment of household goods by cargo plane from Saudi Arabia when he came home on holiday. He had to go back to Lagos to clear the delivery of his goods through customs. Isaac decided to travel to Lagos by public transport as his brother promised to wait for him with a van at the first stop in Lagos. He took the first taxi with six other passengers from Bendel Line taxi station at 6.00 a.m., with the hope of being in Lagos by 10.00 a.m. to do the clearance for the goods. The vehicle was a station wagon type, and the Bendel Line was the state's transport service which was very well-organised and provided the most efficient service at the time. It was about 30 minutes into the journey to the town's outskirts, that highway robbers started to shoot at the vehicle and forced the driver to a stop before he abandoned the vehicle and ran off into the bush.

The passengers were now at the mercy of the robbers, who proceeded to strip them of all their wristwatches, portfolios, suitcases, shoes, cash, and everything possible to steal. They were then ordered out of the vehicles by the 'captain' who was barking orders like a sergeant major. The passengers were told to come out, stand back from the road and put their hands on their heads, which they did very respectfully, even answering the young robbers when directly spoken to with 'Yes, sir.' The robbers ordered Isaac to unclasp his wristwatch from his wrist quickly.

By this time, other motorists had been alerted by witnesses of the start of the robbery, so they were all making U-turns to flee the scene.

The robbers left them standing there while they drove off with the vehicle and all the looted goods. The company sent another vehicle to the passengers and returned them to the station. Isaac did not travel to Lagos that day and he had lost his freight documents. Julie recalls her observation that his portfolio was too heavy, and her advice to decongest it before he went to the bus station. That was when he removed all those documents from his portfolio and left them behind that morning. This had prevented Isaac from losing his British passport, his Saudi Arabia work visa, all his academic certificates, and other important documents. It was a big issue to lose one's passport and try to replace it and the visas quickly. He had to return to Saudi after his holiday, so he needed his passport and visa urgently.

It was about a week after the robbery that Isaac decided to fix the leaking roof of the house, so he stopped at a roadside carpenter's workshop to ask if the boss could take on the 'little' job, but he replied that he had an outside job but that his boys could fix it and promised to send them down on their return from another job. Isaac protested that he wanted the boss himself and did not trust the apprentices because it was a recurring problem after another botched job. The boss now capitulated and promised to stop by later with his boys. They showed up later, and Isaac came out to show them the side of the house with the rotten gutter and leaking roof, leaving them to get on with the job. Isaac came into the house and pulled Julie from the kitchen towards the bedroom, shaking. He could not speak for some minutes from the shock of what he had just seen, and then he said,

'Oh my God, one of the boys was the captain of the armed robbers who attacked us on the highway. He was giving me looks that sent chills through my spine.'

I told him that he was paranoid and that there was no way the young man would have recognised him, but he was convinced that the guy had recognised him or the name from the documents they stole. Isaac came out of the room and became very respectful and generous towards the joiner and his boys, giving them undue praise and a bonus. It turned out that they did a rubbish job, but Isaac did not complain or use their warranty offer, so he did not get them back to fix the problem. Instead, he got an old, experienced man on a recommendation to fix the roof.

Julie and her husband Isaac also lived to tell the tale of a shoot-out with robbers in the same home in Benin City. The evening of the incident started as usual, except that the security guard came in very late that day. Julie knew he was a drunkard who could not resist free drinks at the local bar round the corner if offered to him. He always reeked of alcohol and marijuana. One assumed that he needed to psych himself up for the night job; they had no choice but to keep him, as most of them were the same. Finding someone willing to patrol one's compound solo all night without any guns was not easy. Usually, the guard sits in a little security house with broad windows beside the corner of the gate.

The purpose of having night security guards was to deter trespassers and thieves – not that they have the physical strength or firepower to defend themselves or anyone else. It was just the psychology of the robbers, knowing there was someone there to raise the alarm on intruders.

Usually, they teamed up with their counterparts in other nearby houses and, every hour or so, they blew their whistles or banged some loud, noisy pans to alert each other and keep each other awake. The noise was enough to keep the homeowners awake all night, but one soon got used to it and thought it was normal. The reality is that the feeling of lack of safety was exhausting, and to be on vigil every night was born out of fear and necessity. It is like when Julie first lived near a train line in Northern Ireland; at first, one heard every thundering train go past, but after a while, one soon got accustomed to it and stopped noticing.

Julie and her family were lucky that the robbers were chancers who were not out for a total shoot-out but just out to steal cars. The ones with an ulterior motive to harm the family do not run away. They ambush people or fight at night or even come back with reinforcements at the audacity of the landlord defending his home. Sometimes, they have it in for the homeowner; they bear a grudge or maybe it's just bad luck to come across robbers who feel entitled. One night, Julie was awakened by unusual noises in the compound, so she went around the house to discreet locations to peep out into the compound. That was when she saw the men crawling around the compound. Isaac woke up, took his Dane gun, and shot into the air to frighten them off.

Usually, robbers scramble over the wall and flee after being confronted, so it was a surprise when they fired back twice. Luckily for the family, they did not shoot at the house and scrambled away over the wall. They had started on their mission to remove the two cars in the compound. Usually, in the morning, one found the gate wide open, and the cars gone! Well, the security guard slept through it all because he was inebriated. Everyone suspected that he had been drugged by the robbers at the 'beer parlour' where he usually fuelled himself before resuming work. He admitted that he had accepted many free drinks from some generous revellers that evening.

A beer parlour was usually a shack or a restaurant-style place that served as a pub with food, alcohol and the very potent local gin called 'ogogoro' and palm wine. Ogogoro is the cheapest and most raw locally produced spirit that most people could afford, often putting some in the gutters as early as 8.00 a.m. The production of ogogoro was prohibited by the British during colonial times and labelled 'illicit gin', maybe to stop its competition with imported gin. So, there was the production of alcohol from local sources before the foreigners came to African shores.

It was not always bad things that happened to Julie and her family. Bad news makes better news stories, as good events are happy everyday events like births, weddings, birthday parties and socialising with family and friends. Julie has a large extended family and friends, so invitations never ceased coming in. Nigerians party from Friday evenings to Monday mornings with any excuse. Funerals may be sad, but the burial ceremonies in Benin are huge parties that last for at least three days.

Every opportunity, like weddings, birthday parties and funerals, has given them good reasons to gather.

Patricia Iredia

Chapter 4

TRIBUTES AND REMINISCENCES

Julie makes no claim to fame, only that she lived, loved, served, and did the best she could under every circumstance. As Julie was growing up and all through her adult life, there were people and places that left an indelible mark on her life that she thought of often and would like to remember in her writing so that readers can share in her respect for them. She does not think that her book would be complete without a mention of all the people and places that have had a profound impact on her life, especially now that Covid-19 has taught us that the most important things in life are love, family and friends.

The early years

Julie grew up in a bustling, dusty ancient old city in Nigeria, West Africa, called Benin City and the people are called Edo or Bini people. Benin City is the capital of Edo State of Nigeria. Benin City is famous for its lost bronzes and artefacts that adorn museums worldwide, including the Kelvingrove Museum in Glasgow, Scotland. The first thing that attracted Julie to that part of the museum in Glasgow was when she heard Edo music from a video of the Oba's coronation playing in that corner of the museum amongst several artefacts and modern photographs of Benin. It was poignant to see the centre of Benin City come alive in a museum in Glasgow. The museum in Edinburgh and others worldwide are also home to many of the artefacts from Benin.

The city is famous for its bronze casting and wood carvers along Igun Street. The city used to attract many foreign tourists to see this heritage before the security situation in the country deteriorated in recent years. In 1879, the British raided and trashed the king's palace, taking some artefacts to museums worldwide. Nigeria and Benin have been asking for the return of looted items but without luck yet. In recent times, museums and universities around the world have announced their intention to return some of the stolen bronze castings to Benin.

The palace remains in Benin, and the king, called the 'Oba', still reigns. The story of Benin cannot be complete without mentioning the Oba of Benin and the role he plays in the community's life. It would be like talking about England without a mention of the King and the royal family. The present Oba is Oba Ewuare II, whose coronation was on 20 October 2016. He is the 40th Oba to be crowned in Benin and is passionate about the spiritual and historical importance of the Benin bronzes. Oba Ewuare II demands that they are returned to his people. He has issued a curse against 'juju' priests carrying out human trafficking within his domain to foreign countries and publicly revoked all curses on the victims to release them from the bondage of their 'pimps'. He has also waged war on land grabbers to stop the misery of the citizens who are always exploited and robbed of their lands by unscrupulous community leaders. He has also recently called warring political groups to his palace for reconciliation. His people revere the Oba, and he is the traditional ruler of Benin and the community's spiritual leader.[2]

The palace is a good tourist attraction as there are always traditional activities like parades, dances, and festivals on the grounds all year round. Benin has a lost civilisation recorded in the Guinness World Records book. It described the walls of Benin and its surrounding kingdom as the world's largest earthworks carried out before the mechanical era. Barely any of these walls exist today, but they can still be seen in some areas.[3] Benin is cosmopolitan and traditional, with the centuries-

---

[2] Thomas Imonikhe, 'Oba Ewuare 11: A quintessential monarch at 66', *The Guardian* (18 October 2019): https://guardian.ng/opinion/oba-ewuare-ii-a-quintessential-monarch-at-66/ (accessed 18 March 2021).

[3] Mawuna Koutonin, 'Stories of Cities #5: Benin City, the mighty medieval capital now lost without trace', *The Guardian* (18 March 2016): https://www.theguardian.com/cities/2016/mar/18/story-of-cities-5-benin-city-edo-nigeria-mighty-medieval-capital-lost-without-trace (accessed 20 October 2021).

old Oba's palace at the city's centre. The city centre also boasts a House of Assembly, where legislators meet, and a museum. There is a zoo on the outskirts of town and an airport. Benin is a central hob for all the states of the federation. There are many secondary schools; some used to be run by missionaries, now taken over by the government. Over the years, the government has slowly returned some schools to the churches, and the churches have built new schools. There are three universities in Benin City, the Federal University of Benin and, more recently, two private ones: Igbinedion University and Benson Idahosa University, but Julie attended the premier university of Nigeria, the University of Ibadan, in the west of the country, for her first degree while her Master's and Doctorate degrees were from the Federal University of Benin.

Family

While she was growing up, Julie's parents were Catholic teachers, and her father was a headmaster. He was one of the few monogamous men of his time who married in the church and stayed monogamous throughout his life. 'Baba', as he was called, was a strong disciplinarian and a proven loco parentis to all who got the opportunity to pass under his tutelage. He had some pupils whose parents sent them to live with him to be guided in their learning and disciplined. As a firstborn from a polygamous home, he did not forsake his siblings as he took in all of his brothers and supported their education. Baba taught in many primary, secondary and grammar schools and held high positions in sports and the judiciary as a lay magistrate. He was a geography tutor in the early 1960s at St Maria Goretti Girls' Grammar School in Benin under Sr Henrietta Power.

He left for a brief journey into politics as he was passionate about improving the lives of those in the community. He was elected to the State House of Assembly in 1964, a post he held until 1966, after which he returned to teaching because, in 1966, a military coup ousted them. A unitary military regime came into existence. He was a sharp-shooter and a hunter. This was a sport he enjoyed so much that he spent many weekends away with friends on camping and shooting trips. That generation used to go hunting and fishing, bringing game meat to enrich the family meals.

Baba was the father of eleven girls and one boy, so he was very passionate about girls' education. He was not deterred in his determination to educate his daughters, despite snide remarks from some of his sisters that it was a waste of money to educate girls, 'They should just get married!' they said.

He believed in equality and the right of all children to a good education, and his efforts delivered fruits. Baba's children are all well-educated and successful, which has been passed on to the next generation. He was known as a kind, fair, and honest man in all his jobs and capacity in the judiciary as a Customary Court Judge. He was a teacher first and foremost, then a headteacher, a churchwarden and later an elected member of parliament who had a passion for helping others and fighting for social justice and the common good. Above all these, he was a very loving and caring husband, father, brother and friend.

Julie's mum was a primary school teacher. She spent 35 years teaching before she retired. Meanwhile, she never stopped striving to provide for the family by engaging in various enterprises during the evenings, weekends, and holidays, such as running a groceries kiosk in front of the house where she sold sweets, snacks, beverages, and toiletries. Some snacks were homemade pastries called chin-chin, puff-puff, round doughnuts, and yum-yum doughnuts, all made with flour. Julie credits the shop for her bad teeth because anytime she had to man the shop, she could not resist the temptation to chew the hard sweets very quickly before she was caught eating up all the profits!

All her life, Mum taught children and cared for her brothers and sisters-in-law, nieces, nephews, and grandchildren, which was a remarkable achievement and a huge contribution to humanity. Later in life, she was always a willing babysitter for all her children who needed her. She also supported Baba throughout his teaching career and brief diversion into politics.

Julie was fortunate with the family into which she was born. She grew up in a monogamous home. She has a very close relationship with her siblings, and this has remained a wonder to her friends that they have managed to stay so close, despite being scattered around three continents. Every opportunity, like weddings, birthday parties and funerals, has given them good reasons to gather. They even plan holidays together, such as when 18 family members, including aunties, uncles, nieces and nephews, went on holiday together to Disney Land Florida in 2012. One sister was graduating as a Doctor of Pharmacy, and the whole family were there to support her. Julie lives in Scotland, United Kingdom, and is so glad that she, her daughter, and grandson, could join the party arranged by her sisters, who live in Philadelphia and Nigeria. It was a memorable holiday, especially as it was shared with family. The Disney experience was amazing and will remain with her forever.

Julie gets support from her family, who visit for holidays and show up for weddings, and there is always a listening ear at the end of a phone line. They provided a lot of succour and comfort to her when she was widowed.

The family would meet at the weddings of her nieces and nephews and other family celebrations like 50th, 60th and 70th birthday parties. For her mother's 80th and 90th birthdays, family and friends celebrated with a big party.

Children

Julie believes that her children deserve a special mention because they have all been a source of joy, comfort, and pride to her. They have all stayed on the straight and narrow and are a credit to their parents and society and good role models to the grandchildren and other children growing up in a challenging environment. They have prevailed and succeeded in their quests. They all eventually followed their father into the medical profession, after completing nine first degrees between the five of them. Three are medical doctors, and two are nurses. They never stop working and improving themselves. All of them worked under the challenging situation of being frontline workers during the Covid-19 pandemic, and God saved them and continues to save them. They have shown resilience and discipline and are a credit to their parents, all family, friends, and the community.

They are all married to lovely spouses with 11 grandchildren to keep Julie on her toes, and what wonderful experiences to relive the funny episodes with the grandchildren. One 3-year-old grandson once lay on his back on the grass in a busy park on a sunny day, looking very smug with himself. He folded his hands behind his head as a pillow and looked directly at the sky. Julie asked him, 'What are you doing?'

He lifted his head, looked around with a smile, put his head down and said smugly, 'This is the life.'

The churches and the missionaries

In those days, the Missions built churches and schools in Africa, so there were Baptist, Anglican, and Catholic Missions and missionaries. While Julie was growing up, the church was an integral part of her life. Her nursery, primary and secondary school education were in Catholic schools. Her parents were Catholic teachers who spent much of their time on church activities like being catechism teachers, attending church meetings and planning bazaars. There were the traditional orthodox churches – Catholic, Anglican, and Baptist Missions – besides the practice of traditional religion. The Catholic Church, for example, was most renowned for building schools and hospitals as well as orphanages and old people's homes. These churches significantly impacted education with their missionary schools by supplementing the government efforts. The Catholic

Mission was especially good at providing maternity clinics, care for the elderly, and caring for poor children, supported by nuns, priests and the congregation. Julie was a recipient of Catholic education, from nursery to primary and secondary boarding schools. An Irish nun headed the convent's combined nursery and primary schools, and Catholic priests ran boys' schools. These were very dedicated people to their vocations and they helped to raise a generation of girls and boys in Nigeria. There were other missionary schools in the city, run by the Anglican and Baptist Missions to educate boys and girls. Julie was born in a Catholic maternity hospital called St Philomena. Many nurses and doctors at the time were also nuns and priests supported by African doctors and nurses. Nigerians were running government schools at the same time. The missionary schools were few compared to the number of government schools and were located only in big cities where they greatly impacted education provision.

While the orthodox churches had superiority in providing humanitarian facilities like old people's homes, schools, and hospitals, they did apologise for their role in the beginning during colonisation and the slave trade era. Christians held the Bible in one hand and a gun in the other, but that was centuries ago. Nowadays, they certainly concentrate on the spiritual side of their mission. Over the past 50 years, a new wave of religion swept into the city and the country. The new age churches brought the advent of Evangelicals infiltrating from America's mega-churches. The age of 'prosperity' preachers arrived. They were fascinating and had successful superstar aura around them. They were dubbed 'prosperity' preachers because they focused a lot on the word prosperity, almost as if poverty was a crime and everyone had to be materially rich to serve God well. This message was in sharp contrast to the content of orthodox churches that preached peace, hope and the love of Christ as a panacea for all problems rather than emphasising material gratification.

When Julie was about 15 years old, she lost her best friend, who lived opposite her, to one of the new churches. Her friend did not want to fraternise with her anymore because she was not a 'born again' Christian, whatever that meant. The phrase 'born again' is still a very contentious term to the ordinary person. Does it mean that Christians practising their faith in other churches are not born again, as in baptised by the Holy Spirit? Julie did not support or join her by covering her hair and spending every available moment in the church on one prayer activity or another.

In the beginning, the new churches were very judgemental of older churches, claiming that their brand of Christianity was better. Julie was perplexed because she felt that churches should spend their time converting the 'unbeliever' rather than wasting time slagging each other off. With time, though, they have calmed down and become mainstream with a vast following while other smaller churches have sprung up, sometimes in every other house on a street in some areas of her town. Julie's friend did relax after some years and started to uncover her hair and even apply make-up to her face and stopped being so judgemental, which was a sign that her church had moved on and brought them back to the mainstream.

Sister Henrietta Power, OLA

The Reverend Sister Henrietta Power was the first principal of Julie's secondary school in Benin City, where she was a boarder from age 11 to 17. Sister Henrietta was a visionary teacher whose challenge was to produce girls who could hold their own in any profession. She smashed barriers that had existed at that time. She got to Nigeria at age 25 and did not leave until retirement at 77. She died in a retirement convent in Ireland on 30 November 2020 at the age of 97. Her funeral was attended on Zoom by 'her girls' from all over the world.

In those days, many foreign teachers were around, especially missionaries. There were also mathematics and science teachers recruited from the Indian subcontinent. The nuns in Julie's Catholic school taught curriculum subjects like maths and chemistry, as well as love, compassion, and propriety. Sister Henrietta herself was a chemistry graduate from an Irish university. Like her, all the nuns deemed girls' education to be paramount for self-dependency in the future. They practised their vocation with diligence, dedication, and devotion to duty, to a very high admirable standard.

Boarding school was very regimented, between morning assembly, mass, classes, siesta, prep, meals, and sleep, and repeated all over again every day. There were also external activities like going to the stadium for inter-school games or being selected to attend inter-house school sports days, school debates and visits to orphanages or other religious obligations. The school was home away from home, and Sister Henrietta and other staff made sure they had a memorable experience in and out of the classroom. Julie remembers that 'Sister', as she was called, took care of their academic needs and emotional, psychological, and physical well-being.

Julie remembers how petrified the girls were about 'lady koi koi'. The girls thought that every night at about 2.00 a.m. in the dormitory, they could hear the repeated sound of 'koi koi'; it was like a spooky haunted house. Julie was frozen in bed, afraid to move or even breathe. She remembers Sister reassuring them by making a show of bringing holy water to sprinkle everywhere and her coming over at different times of the night, just walking around. That was very reassuring for the young minds. Later in adult life, the former students speculated that it could have been some noise from a factory nearby, unless one believed in ghosts!

Julie first encountered Sister Henrietta Power in 1967, when she ended up in St Maria Goretti Girls' Grammar School in Benin City. Before then, she had been away at boarding school at Mary Mount College, Agbor, one hour away from Benin City. On the day the Nigerian Civil War broke out, the students were lined up by Sister Perpetua, the head teacher. She shepherded them into hired vehicles that took them to their different destinations home. They never returned to their old school because the war raged for another two and a half years. All the girls who returned home from Catholic schools were automatically absorbed into St Maria Goretti, Benin, to replace the girls who had hurriedly left to enter the rebel territory where their families lived. So, Julie started at the new school in July 1967.

That was the beginning of her association with this remarkable woman who profoundly affected the lives of the girls who crossed her path. She had a knack for raising young girls and nurturing them to achieve their best potential. She was far ahead of her time and taught life and vocational skills beyond the curriculum. Sister Henrietta brought in local craftsmen to teach weaving, tailoring, embroidery, and cookery at a time when these were not on the School Board's curriculum. Many of the girls still have the pieces of embroidery and cane work hanging proudly in their parents' homes. Julie made a jewellery basket lined with pink satin that is still in her mother's display cabinet.

The girls used to turn out in well-ironed navy-blue pinafore uniforms with clean white shirts and, every Monday morning, went through military-style inspection at the school assembly. Sister Henrietta never relapsed on her standard when it came to neatness. Also, she would gather all the children from the neighbouring villages, give them a simple maths and English test, and from there, she awarded full scholarships to the selected kids. These children would turn up without shoes on their feet, but Sister knew how to select those who had potential with their ability in maths, if not English. These were disadvantaged children from impoverished homes. Sister Henrietta paid all their bills, including the supply of uniforms and books. Many of them went on to do great things. The school was in a village previously located on the outskirts of the town, but today it has become part of the town as it has grown.

Julie remembers Sister Henrietta in class teaching manners and etiquette. When a teacher was absent from class, she would come in, and, on that day, you knew you would learn something new. She remembers the day the lesson was 'Yes, I mind' and 'No, I don't mind.' Another day, it was a short discussion on 'Whose job is harder, the man who works in an office as the boss or the one who does physical labourer work?' They learned then to view all sides of a debate critically and to see that there are always complex issues on each side of the debate. She also remembers Sister Henrietta on the school bus from Benin to Lagos with some six students she had selected to travel with her. She was on her way to trade in the school bus for a bigger 18-seater one. They sang all the way to Lagos and, when they got there, stayed in a Catholic boarding school for girls in Maryland, from where they went to watch the film *My Fair Lady* at the cinema in 1968. These are just a few examples of the memories that Sister Henrietta created.

She would stimulate your mind, and for days and years later, you could still remember all the dilemmas and solutions she shared. She had absolute confidence in her belief that she could make a difference in the lives of girls and that they could do anything they set out to do, and they did. The school had a reputation for producing well-rounded, well-mannered, competent girls. They were always the first choice for wife seekers, university admissions, and employers. The girls did well.

Sister Henrietta was a good woman, firm but gentle, demanding but kind, talented, and an excellent administrator. She is still held in very high esteem and affection by all who crossed her path. The old girls' association named the new hall after her, and many delegations went to visit her in her nursing home in

Ireland. She left an indelible mark in the hearts and minds of all who crossed her path. Was she a visionary teacher? Yes, she was, to the extent that promoting excellence was the only thing good enough for her girls. This tribute to Sister Henrietta Power is a testament to the positive impact she had on the lives of the girls who crossed her path. She received the 'Order of Niger' award from the Nigerian government for advancing girls' education in Nigeria and her services to the country. The University of Benin also gave her an honorary doctorate. She was in Nigeria in the era of missionary workers of all denominations, but her longevity and dedication to duty were second to none. Rest in peace, Sister Henrietta.

University days

Julie's generation was the generation that had it good in Nigeria. They were dubbed 'the oil-boom generation' by historians and journalists. Her generation had bursary awards at university and heavily subsidised meals at the cafeteria. The government got a lot of oil revenue which they promptly squandered on festivals like the Festival of Arts and Culture 1977 (FESTAC 77) and excessive spending on contracts and bureaucracies. The cultural show had its benefits by bringing artists from all over the world to showcase African music, fine art, literature, drama, dance, and religion, but critics pointed to the colossal amount that was spent. The FESTAC estate is still being used as housing for various families who bought the houses, so that was a good outcome.

The 1970s was a great time to be a young person in Nigeria. The country was full of hope and optimism, and the university students like Julie could travel to London during the summer holidays to do summer jobs and save money.

Julie always wished she had studied Education at university for her first degree instead of Language Arts as she now had to do a postgraduate diploma in Education soon after. A degree in Education would have meant receiving a very generous bursary from the federal government, which had a special scheme to train teachers. Her teacher parents would not have had to sponsor her education by collecting money from her two working sisters, to which they would add and then send postal orders via the post office monthly to cover fees. They never failed to send Julie money throughout her time at university. Moreover, she would not have needed to study a postgraduate course in Education. At the time, she was leaning towards journalism as a possible career but changed her mind when she landed a job in the Civil Service as an education officer soon after graduating. This role included being part of school inspection teams and implementing government policies at all levels of education. Julie's generation was the last set that got a job for life and easily got loans for cars and housing. Nowadays, unemployment is the bane of society, and Nigeria is not a welfare state, so one wonders how people manage to survive daily.

University days were the experimental years when it was assumed that one tried everything. One would be lucky if one did not attend parties where it was evident from the start that something was wrong. Julie attended one such party. It was graduation season, and many students were holding parties in various locations around the campus.

The party in question was touted as an exclusive PhD graduation party at the university club complex, which made Julie and her friends feel very privileged to have been invited. They had been to parties there in the past, and their food and music were great. That venue was famous for hosting posh events because a jazz band was always in attendance in the background. The bar was always open right next door with 'suya' being cooked on the spot (a Nigerian spiced barbecued beef, chicken, or lamb on skewers).

They thought the party was going to take place in one of the open reception rooms or conference rooms, and it never occurred to them that the party was in a private suite occupied by a guest in one of the guest houses. As soon as they arrived and were heralded to the room, it all seemed very odd. Even though they entered the premises through the reception at the front, they ended up outside the building through the back door into another building housing guest houses. Julie asked her friend Helen who had invited them, 'Is it a room party we came here for?' She too was surprised.

The men had a habit of begging their friends who were girls to help them recruit girls to a party. Parties and dances were deemed unsuccessful if boys seriously outnumbered the girls. Julie's friend apologised that she thought the party was in one of the reception rooms in the lobby area. The room was dim, dark, and smoky, and one could hardly make out any faces; only white teeth could be seen. Julie also smelt some 'leafy' aroma (possibly marijuana) in the air, mixed with a strong smell of alcohol, and the space was too small for the number of people sandwiched in there. Julie and one of her friends instinctively ran out of the room into the open air between the buildings. They were followed out by two of the young men, but no amount of pleading would make Julie and her friend go back in there. It is always wise to follow one's instinct in situations like this without hesitation.

She left the party with her friend and went to another graduation party that was taking place in a reception room at their hall of residence. They had been invited to many graduation parties that day. Julie was not surprised to hear stories and rumours later that, at the club party, drinks were spiked, date rape drugs were used to drug some girls, and they were gang raped. The perpetrators got away with it because the police in Nigeria at that time (and even at present) did not have the facilities for testing for drugs or doing DNA tests. Nor were they even interested in proving anything, as they saw the girls as 'voluntary' participants by just being there. That was the attitude of the police in those days, so it was a girl's responsibility to mind her company and her whereabouts. Accusing someone of rape and being able to prove it is daunting in any country in the world, even now.

When Julie tried smoking a cigarette at university, the experience was so repulsive that she never repeated the trial. She felt it was an overrated experience. The smoke made her splutter and cough, but she had friends who enjoyed smoking who told her she did not know what she was missing. Julie decided that smoking was an acquired taste and not for her. Smoking was part of the dating scene then and was one of the ways to assert that one had 'arrived', meaning that one was posh and sophisticated. Julie had her share of 'dating' while growing up, but the only notable story was about the guy whose father wanted to murder her. He decided that he hated girls from her tribe and that his son was never to bring home a girl from Benin. He was from another tribe less than an hour from Benin with a different language, so it was not a personal thing against Julie. He hated her tribe amongst whom he lived and from whom he made his money.

When her friend at the time took her home, on seeing them, his father started shouting that they should get out of his compound. Otherwise, he would go inside and bring a gun to shoot her dead. He angrily sprang out of his chair on the veranda, where he was enjoying the fresh air, and walked back inside. Julie had not been aware of an issue with his dad, which he thought he had fixed. That relationship stood no chance of surviving with a father like that who was issuing all sorts of threats. Some people like that always felt that they could rule over others because they had age, money, and privilege on their side then. It was a terrifying experience.

Julie remembers her university days for some activities which caught her attention; the 'pirates' on campus and the killing of students by the military government for demonstrating against increases in university fees. 1978 saw one of the most violent student demonstrations in Nigeria under the Mohammed and Obasanjo administration. It was dubbed the 'Ali must go' demonstration by students. A student at the University of Lagos was shot dead by the police. The shooting infuriated students all over the country. Students went on a rampage. Violent protests led to the killing by soldiers of eight more students at Zaria, leaving many others injured. The universities were closed, and students were sent home for a while. When the university was re-opened, Julie completed her degree examinations and graduated that year, 1978.

The Pirates, like some other rival clubs, were a 'cult' with only the members knowing what their ethos or manifesto was, but they were feared by non-members, especially females who came across them at night when they were 'sailing'. Julie and her friends once came across them at 2.00 a.m. as they were heading to their hall of residence, having left the faculty of Arts after studying for final exams. It is well known that no one should be out when the Pirates were 'out'. It was a very frightening experience as all the girls huddled together for their dear lives. Despite all the rumours and hype, the most terrible thing that happened to them that night was being escorted by singing 'louts' to their doorstep. They belted out songs like 'The pirates are sailing, and you dare to be out … you are joking with us …' in a laddish manner.

Clubs were part of the culture of university life; the 'cults' and the palm wine drinkers' club mixed with the gentlemen's club that invited the girls to tuxedo and evening-wear dinner dances, and the disco maniacs who hit the nightclubs every weekend. There was a niche for everyone. Unfortunately, this cult culture has now acquired a violent dimension. The authorities are now accusing secondary school children and university students of rival killings in the name of cultism, whatever that represents.

Early working life

It is a miracle that Julie did not end up as a gambler because her first job was in a betting house when she was 15 years old. In Nigeria, Julie's family home was in a very cosmopolitan part of town and close to the biggest market in Benin, so it was not unusual to find business premises dotted among residential homes. Lebanese businesspeople were running the gambling business in a two-storey building across the street from Julie's home. The gambling was pools betting, based on Premier League matches in the UK and other European championships. On Saturday evenings, all the betting cards had to be checked manually to find out who had predicted the results of matches correctly and won a prize. It was a very tense working environment, with supervisors breathing down staff members' necks to prevent people from marking the cards.

It was the school holidays, and the kids were back home from boarding school. Julie's mum reckoned that she could get two or three kids into this holiday weekend job that paid quite well. That money was beneficial as she had a lot of mouths to feed and bodies to clothe, and she loved challenges. The Lebanese man did not bother asking for their ages because he was simply happy to help a 'good' family from the neighbourhood, and these were children he could trust not to be dodgy with the cards. The adults there were displeased that children were taking their jobs and gave them daggered looks because some adults were turned away on the day.

It was a decent work experience as it taught them discipline and responsibility. Julie remembers that the job involved speed and some calculations. Her dad played the pools, but it had never occurred to Julie that children could try it. She was proud to have a Saturday job and earn money which was a rare novelty then.

Julie finished secondary school at 18 after her A-level examinations. Before going to the university, she worked as a bank clerk for some months in the summer. They did not appreciate it when Julie left after a few months for the university after all the training received. They thought she would stay and rise through the ranks and become a bank supervisor, as most women did then. Julie was one of the trailblazers of her time, with many young women aspiring to higher education rather than settling for jobs with no degrees.

Undergraduates in Nigeria then had many opportunities to work during the long summer holidays. Julie was lucky to get a temporary job at her former bank in the first year. The second year saw the birth of the federal government initiative 'Operation Feed the Nation' (OFN). Every free plot of land was to become a farm or a vegetable patch. Every school was ordered to turn their empty lands or gardens into mini farms to grow food during agriculture lessons. As with all the lofty initiatives, it was phenomenally successful for a while. The federal government demonstrated that farming was profitable when done correctly with fertilisers. The idea was to diversify the economy from sole reliance on oil. Growing food was a priority to feed the millions in the country. Julie worked on a school farm and was pleasantly surprised to find that she enjoyed the experience of planting crops, harvesting corn in season, and taking plenty of vegetables home to her mum. Unfortunately, the governments kept changing and these initiatives were not followed through by successive administrations. It collapsed after a few years.

Many students travelled to the UK and worked for agencies that recruited people to do hospitality jobs. Julie spent her last undergraduate summer holiday in London as a catering assistant at the post office and a kitchen assistant in a hospital.

Every graduate in Nigeria must do National Service for a year, a mandate that started in 1973, and this applies to all graduates of universities and polytechnics. Julie was deployed to Plateau State in the Middle Belt, where she taught English to secondary school students. The project achieved its goal of uniting the country and allowing people to experience another part of the country where one would never have travelled to. It was an incredibly liberating experience.

Julie came back home from Northern Nigeria and settled into a job as a civil servant in the Education department of the state's Ministry of Education, Bendel State (now Edo State). After three years in this role, Julie emigrated to the UK to be with her husband.

Marital life

Julie married a dashing young man called Isaac when she was 25 years old. Everyone said he came from London, but actually, he came from Belfast in Northern Ireland, where he was a trainee doctor. He came home to attend his sister's wedding. Julie and her sister were very involved in the wedding preparations as they had all been classmates at secondary school, and Julie's sister was the chief bridesmaid. It was a case of:

'Who is this?'

'Meet my brother Isaac. He arrived yesterday from the UK for my wedding.'

'This is my friend Julie.'

Julie stretched out her hand and replied, 'Pleased to meet you.'

The rest is history.

There were no mobile phones then, so young men simply showed up on one's doorstep for a visit if they were interested in you. Naturally, some got invited in, and some had the door slammed in their faces. Isaac was lucky to be invited in, which was the beginning of the relationship that led to a wedding 18 months later. It was the best decision she ever made because he turned out to be a 'perfect' friend and husband and the best father any child could have. He was a kind, generous, and loving soul.

Julie relocated to the UK and had two babies in quick succession. She moved from Africa to a different country with a completely different culture (although she had previously visited during the summer holidays to work.) Living in a different culture meant isolation and loneliness, as you are without family and friends dropping by. Julie soon settled into her studies at the university and made new friends. Her husband was thoughtful enough to arrange for her to start a course immediately she arrived, before the babies came along.

Attending a course helped her to acclimatise and make friends. He knew she liked academics and would have been bored alone at home all day. At that time, junior doctors worked crazy hours. Being on call for a weekend meant leaving for work on Friday morning and returning home on Monday evening.

The choice of a postgraduate education course was because they always planned to return to Africa as soon as Isaac completed his specialist training. Julie had been an education officer before coming to the UK. In fact, she did the course on in-service training from her employers, the Ministry of Education, and they paid the fees.

They did go back 'home' to Nigeria when he got a job at a new University Medical School, but soon after, the military government shut it down after a coup. He was in limbo again, so he started a private clinic in Benin that expanded to become a hospital with other doctors working there. He then worked in the UK and Saudi Arabia for some years while the rest of the family lived in Nigeria. They were soon back in the UK while he worked out the options for the future, but they never returned. They remained unsettled until they came to Scotland in 1996 and settled on the Isle of Lewis. Julie delivered her children in Northern Ireland, Wales, and three in England, such was their itinerant life.

Julie adapted very quickly to the way of life on the island; coffee mornings with friends, helping on gala days with hair braiding, volunteering in the primary school library and on school trips. Life became settled even though Julie always wondered if she would ever be able to work again. Julie missed being at work, a very different experience from being a full-time housewife. Looking after her family was a full-time occupation, and Julie could not afford the time to go out to work, but that did not stop the wishful thinking that she could have a semblance of her old life. She was the corporate type at heart and never fancied herself as a domestic goddess, but that was her only viable option on an island in a family of seven. Julie soon got used to it.

Education gives one the credentials and confidence to go out into the world of work and seek a 9.00–5.00 job. That was the 'ideal' scenario for some, but life does not always follow that stereotypical path. Sometimes, one's degrees don't lead to corporate jobs but are valuable and productive in other occupations. Two of her sisters have degrees in Education and Law, but today they are self-employed as fashion designers. Sometimes, it was difficult for Julie to answer questions like: 'What are you doing now?'

When you tell them what you do, they ask, 'So, you are just a housewife?'

Some of her friends and acquaintances are very intolerant of what they perceive to be different from the norm. The idea of not being in a 9.00–5.00 employment or having salaried work is alien to some. One sometimes gets snide remarks based on assumptions that one is doing 'nothing', like: 'What exactly do you do?'

When one says what one does, such as 'I run a business from home' or 'I'm writing a book', you are not believed. Sometimes you are mocked.

One cannot win the arguments, so it is best to concentrate on living one's own life as one sees fit. Julie has realised that one does not owe anyone any justification or explanation for one's life choices. All these dramatic changes happened in Julie's life when she got married. She left her Civil Service job behind, relocated to the United Kingdom, had five children, lived on an island, and stayed at home, putting her career on the back burner and becoming a homemaker. Julie became a widow after the unfortunate passing of her husband after a brief illness. Julie got all her encouragement from her children, family, friends, church members and some unexpected quarters. This encouragement helped her be happy with her life and concentrate on what she could do. She tried to appreciate the opportunities available to her in all spheres of life at different stages. Take writing; for example, one can try being a writer from one's bedroom. All that is needed is a laptop and the will to do it. One can also run a business from home. Online business offers many possibilities, such as buying and selling for those so inclined. But she engaged in property management, trading in shares, and goods.

Julie pays tribute to her late husband, Isaac, for all she has been able to accomplish since he has been gone. He was a very thoughtful, disciplined, and loving husband and father. His love for his family made raising stable, confident, ambitious, and achieving children possible. The stories he told them about resilience and success, his demeanour and fairness have left a legacy of well-balanced children. He left them with a roof over their heads and the confidence to face the future without worries. Julie credits Isaac with the ability to complete her PhD because anytime she remembered his dedication and contribution to the work, she felt compelled to re-start and finish it.

The story started when they arrived back in Britain in July 1996. The destination was a Scottish island, but he had arranged for them to stay one week in London because he wanted the children to have a holiday as it was the summer holidays and schools were closed. They were typical tourists with plenty of time to spare, visiting attractions such as Buckingham Palace, Madame Tussauds, London Zoo, the Trocadero, and Trafalgar Square. They also spent the evenings visiting family all over London. It was not until they got to their hotel that they realised they were missing a hand luggage-sized suitcase containing all of Julie's PhD materials.

In those days, folks used long-hand and typewriters to write their essays. One had to hire a typist and go backwards and forwards to get it typed and corrected. Julie's husband, Isaac, had typed the final copy, and she was waiting for it to go to the external examiner. However, first, she had to effect all the corrections demanded at the viva, and present that to the departmental supervisor, get the changes approved before copies were made and sent out to external examiners. That was when she packed to return to Britain, and the bag got lost.

Julie underestimated what it would mean to move with five school-aged children. The loss of her work grieved her. She thought of recovering an old copy from her supervisor but all her personal notes and corrections in the copy would be missing. She quickly became overwhelmed by the immediate problems of running a family of seven. Isaac never gave up, as the kind and considerate man he was; he went looking for the bag when he went to London for a conference three years after it got lost. He remembered that when they got off the Heathrow train at Caledonian Road tube station, they took a bus to the B&B which he had booked nearby, and he had always counted the suitcases before then. He went to the London Transport 'Lost Property' office, where he miraculously found the bag, after describing it and giving the date it went missing. Before then, the London office always claimed over the phone not to have it. It was unbelievable when he walked in with the suitcase. He was so attached to the work because he had typed most of it and was very familiar with it. He contacted her supervisor, but the statutory time and the logistics were against her. She put it to the back of her mind until after she was widowed in 2004.

On being widowed, her first instinct was to want to return home to her mother and her family. She did not realise that that was all part of the grieving process. Coincidentally, her supervisor contacted her and told her that there was a moratorium, suspending deadlines for students to complete their PhD programmes. He would like Julie to re-apply to the university to complete her work. She wanted to complete it for Isaac because he had typed the entire last copy, and he always felt guilty and sorry that she had not climbed the final hurdle. He felt he had robbed her by moving the family at that time, but that was a family decision, and she soon forgot about it, or rather, she put it to the back of her mind, which was a better description. Who could forget five years of grilling and a completely written-up PhD that did not jump the final hurdle?

Life on an island

Life took on its routine, which revolved around husband and children and their activities. Julie made some good friends who invited her for coffee mornings or lunches when the children were in school. The family also had group activities with other families from the church, like going to the beach or having church parties to mark historic days like Burns Night and Bonfire Night. Julie remembers her family turning up at the first Bonfire Night without fireworks or food. They soon learned. Burns Night used to be celebrated after mass in the parish house with a potluck dinner, and everyone brought food to share.

All the members always ended up on the beach later for a barbecue. They loved walking the long beach stretches and exploring caves by the beach. Julie fell in love with Scottish music on the island, and two of her children went to highland dancing classes; some took part in Gaelic plays at school and got the loudest ovations for speaking the local language. The headteacher used to transcribe the script for them. Years of Ceilidh dancing on the island has turned Julie into a lover of bagpipe music, which she often plays on 'Alexa' while cooking in her kitchen in Glasgow. She also remembers her home in Africa by playing Afro music in every genre. African gospel music can be very inspiring.

Being a homemaker and volunteering were delightful times in Julie's life when the children were growing up. Life revolved around the family and all their school and extra-curricular activities. She also volunteered in the school library and on school trips and gala days. After being widowed, she volunteered in the Day Care Centre, helping to look after the elderly who came to do activities organised by the centre. While she was volunteering in the day centre, the boss saw her one day and told her to go to the home for adults with learning disabilities, be a worker there and get paid. That was a very compassionate thing for the boss to have done. Julie worked there for about two and a half years while waiting for the last two of her children to finish secondary school.

Life as a widow

Many things changed when her husband died, and her life turned upside down. Julie now appreciated the life she had more than she did before. She realised that love and family were the most important things in her life, which have never changed. She had lived a very sheltered and privileged life, never having to worry about money, and her life had been safe, secure, full of love and appreciation, and well worth all the sacrifices made. She had a corporate job before ending up on an island. Julie sometimes felt that her choices in life were being questioned by some people when they negatively said, 'You are just a housewife?'

Surely, no one has a right to judge another's priorities in life, as we do not walk in another's shoes. An easier question is, 'Did you have a good life?'

She felt lucky to have had a husband who understood her dilemma and involved her in all his enterprises to give her life some meaning outside of children's school homework and domestic chores. She developed skills which became useful when she found herself a widow at 49. For example, he loved to invest in shares and properties, and he taught her that. Julie's answer to the question above is that she has had a good life.

Life took a terrible turn in her psyche when her husband died after a brief illness. Julie was lucky that two of her children were already away from home at the university on the mainland, and the others had grown up a bit by then. The last two were 14 and 15 years old. Julie remembers the day his well-meaning boss came around and advised that they might have to downsize. One would like to say that he was quite pleasantly surprised to hear that Isaac had taken care of his family's future. He had fully paid off his mortgage and made financial arrangements to take care of his family. They did not have to worry about how to downsize, move house and survive. Knowing that his family's future was secure, Isaac was very happy. However, he wished he could be around to see his children grow up. Nothing would have made him sadder when ill than if his family were left homeless and in need of instant help. During the closing hours, all he worried about was his family, asking all his closest relatives to please take care of his children, to be there for them when they needed a father. That is a testament to the kind of man he was, selfless and compassionate.

Being a mother of five, a full-time housewife and a carer for her husband in the end, had given Julie a hectic life. After his tragic death, she remained on the island for three years while her children finished their secondary education before relocating to Glasgow. Julie found it an exceedingly difficult time in her life. Being widowed makes one re-examine one's life. Everything is different, and your social life takes a heavy knock. No more couple outings, no more corporate parties, and conferences. Some friends still invited her to their homes and visited her, always bearing gifts. Julie and Isaac had booked to attend the Obstetricians' and Gynaecologists' Congress in Australia (two years later) while attending the one hosted in Harrogate, England, but that was not to be as he fell ill in the interim.

Julie realised that, for most of her adult life in the UK, she had been emotionally and financially dependent on Isaac, but in her case, not in a bad way. She earned her stay in the partnership, which was their understanding of marriage and togetherness, but life would have been scary and empty but for the children, family, and good friends. Friends were extremely helpful and made life easier for Julie, especially when she had to abandon the children at home to follow Isaac to treatment regimes in Glasgow, sometimes for more than a week, especially at the beginning.

Where could she begin again to rebuild her life? She volunteered in a Day Care Centre where she was involved in helping the elderly with daytime entertainment, meals, and excursions. She derived immense pleasure from doing this and learnt to knit from the ladies. It was fascinating to have a glimpse into old age in the future, which will inevitably come to every one of us. Julie remembers how often she had to throw card games to make the old folks win and be happy with their achievement. She later went to work in a home for adults with learning disabilities. It was a life saver to have somewhere to go, something to do and to make friends.

They were a very sociable group with many ceilidh nights where Julie was 'forced' to learn the dances. She had a good time doing that job.

How to navigate widowhood

It is challenging to maintain friendships with men as a widow, no matter how close to you they were when your husband was alive. As soon as it happened, many people offered to help, especially by taking the children to places, and they kept their promises to help. Julie will be forever grateful to everyone who came to the aid of the family. Julie was very quick to realise that, despite all their good intentions, she had to put a brake on the need to ask for help eventually.

Other widows told her horror stories of the attitude of some wives when their husbands were helping a widow out, and Julie realised that she may have been at the receiving end of that. One widow told her how her husband's best friend was helping with the children's school run just after her husband died. Then one day, she got a visit from his wife to warn her off asking for help from her husband. The wife said, 'You keep calling him uncle, uncle, and then one day he will be in your bed.'

Her widowed friend stopped accepting his help from that very day, to his utter shock. It is up to the new widow to quickly snap out of the 'dependence' phase and realise that she must embrace this new life with all the hardships it brings. It always gets easier. It was shocking to Julie that anyone could be so mean and insensitive, but that is one of the lessons a widow must learn, who to accept help from and who to keep at bay.

Something like that widow's experience also happened to Julie, so it might be widespread to be warned by a friend's wife that the widow should keep away from her husband. The warning came in snide remarks like, 'Every woman should have the privilege to enjoy their own husband until the end.' It does not matter what promises he made to his late friend to help his family, problems will come from his wife, and even neighbours and onlookers would start gossiping that 'something could be happening' when it was all perfectly innocent. Some people may not accept that a man and a woman can be just friends without ulterior motives. Being a young widow with young children can expose one to indignities that one may not suffer otherwise, as one is very vulnerable and dependent on friends. After the mandatory mourning period, plan for your children's transportation to places wherever possible and limit physical contact with male helpers to avoid suspicion and awkward situations later.

Good financial planning is essential. Hindsight is perfect, but how many couples plan together for future eventualities when there is no problem? – but they should, and some do. If planning was not possible when the man was alive, then it is essential to consider the long-term plans made by the widow. Explore all the possibilities rationally. Re-train if you can and re-enter the job market if not already in it. Just keep busy in any shape or guise to maintain one's mental health. In the UK, one can volunteer while deciding what to do next or as a step toward getting into a particular employment. If, for whatever reason, one is not in a state of mind to study or work, do not be afraid or embarrassed to ask for help from the relevant agencies.

Julie once came across a doctor who told her that she had lost her husband before she could even take her examinations for working in the UK and was stuck with four children, two of whom she had sent back to her aged mother in Nigeria. She could hardly feed herself and provide for her children and was close to a mental health breakdown. This widow was relatively new to living in the UK as her late husband had come first, so she did not know where to turn, or thought that seeking help was not for people like her. She should be working, she thought. Another widow from her church convinced that widow to go to the council for help. That was a turning point; she got help with her rent and the children, and her fears and anxieties were reduced. Later, she was able to bring the two children back from Nigeria. She made it. Julie was lucky not to have gone through what that widow went through because Isaac had sorted everything out.

Today, she is a practising doctor in the UK and giving back to the system. Widows, please do not be embarrassed to seek help. There are local government agencies and charitable organisations out there that help widows.

It is asserted that being religious can help people cope with widowhood, and Julie believes this. Many religions preach faith in God, hope and love. For example. Christians believe that God is the father of the fatherless, the friend, and the widow's husband, and that belief in God creates peace of mind that passes human understanding. Those who practise their faith tend to have more resilience and coping strategies. Being prayerful helps one to put life into perspective by believing in God to help one through difficult situations.

For example, for widows who attend church, this is the time to join some organisations within the church. Sometimes this helps us remove all attention from the self and focus on other issues, like the St Vincent de Paul Society in the Catholic Church, which focuses on helping the poor. The church can provide an avenue for worship, spiritual uplift, and physical and emotional help. It can also provide a social life as one meets many people, makes friends, and participates in various activities in and outside the church.

Always try to limit what regrets you have. Do the best you can and be happy with yourself, do not live a life of regrets, as this is pointless; we are only here for a time. Do not compare yourself to or compete with anyone, do what makes you happy and fulfilled and do what you can. Do not even compare yourself to another widow or let someone else tell you to emulate another widow. Sometimes a widow is advised to move on and imitate those who have re-married or have a new partner. Do not be made to feel guilty for not being so inclined. No one knows what your priorities or your needs are but yourself. Do things at your own pace, especially when children are involved. Socialise as much as possible through group activities such as church events and attending friends' parties. It can be difficult if one has been used to couple events and socials.

It is time to embrace the single life by joining groups where one can be an individual. Here in the UK, there are widows' and widowers' meet-up groups where one can be with people who have experienced similar grief. It is an excellent social network packed with many activities, and Julie did just that. There are also women's groups to meet every need – for example, African and Caribbean Women's Organisations with their support network. Joining a group can open opportunities for friendships, support, and even jobs.

Be strong when it comes to the discipline of children. Maintaining discipline is one of the hardest aspects of being a widow raising children alone. It is challenging even for two people, so maintaining discipline alone is arduous. It is very tempting to become over-generous to the children or over-indulge them because one feels sorry for them for having no father. The widow must toughen up and discipline the children. Do not be blackmailed into letting them misbehave or become over-demanding. Present a firm exterior and develop the moral authority to demand resilience from them. At this time, the stakes are higher for them to succeed. There is no father to guide them. Teach them to be strong by giving them assignments that demand strength. They should help with chores like cooking, mowing the grass, cleaning, and taking out the bins. One must not forget extra-curricular activities like sports and music to help them relax and meet others. They should be encouraged to keep good friends and do well in school. They can also be brought up with religious values if one is religious. It helps to teach children values and virtues in trying to obey the Ten Commandments in the Bible. Anyone that can do that will be a winner!

At this time, especially at the beginning, one might feel worthless and surplus, as husbands could be demanding when around! For those used to being at the constant service of another, do not replace the gap created by the loss with accepting unhealthy relationships. Do not cling to disrespectful relationships you would never have had if you had not been widowed. Do not accept or prolong abusive relationships in any guise. Free yourself from toxic relationships and focus on yourself, your children, and the things that make you happy, not on what anyone else expects.

Be guided by your strength, needs, priorities, values and, above all, instincts. Make mistakes, turn back when you can, and move on. To understand this simple principle, imagine a car driver controlled by the passenger, who may be the boss, friend, or family. Some passengers will continually comment on how the driver is driving. They say things like, 'Why are you wasting time?– there was a gap right there, and you did not enter the highway. Oh no, you should not go that way, turn left, turn right, that road is quicker!' even though the driver knows the destination they are heading to and how to get there.

The continued interruption of the passenger can lead to a crash if care is not taken. A driver cannot drive with the judgement of a passenger. The driver must use their own perceptions and timing when driving. While at the junction, the driver must move when they feel safe, not when someone else thinks they should. This principle is true of life as well. This journey through life is not a race that must adhere to Olympics rules. Do things when you are ready. Run your race while focusing on your priorities of providing and protecting yourself and your loved ones.

Fights over properties are often an issue in our Nigerian culture for the widow because there is so much confusion about the interpretation of inheritance rules. These are not legal but cultural, as one must go to a legal court for redress if one is unhappy with the local culture affecting the widow. Unlike the Western world, inheritance culture is quite different for different communities in Nigeria, and the interpretation can be open to corruption and falsehoods. There are cases of widows driven out of their matrimonial homes with young children because their late husband supposedly had a son by a girlfriend (no DNA proof of being his son!) before he married his wife.

A couple may have started together with nothing and then become millionaires, but in some cultures, the woman could still be left with nothing at the appearance of a first 'son' on the scene. Such things happen in cases where the man has invested all the assets in only his name. Wives are sometimes scared to mention the word 'will' to protect themselves and their kids for fear of being accused of wanting the man dead.

Some African cultures relish the punishment of widows as they are often thought responsible for their husband's death, even in this twenty-first century. Women, please be advised to protect yourselves financially while the man is still alive because an older son than yours can come out of the woodwork after his passing. If the man will not share his property with his wife while he is still alive or act to protect her and the children, then one cannot blame the antics of relatives later as they have the power to share the property as they deem fit with nothing for the widow! The courts supersede traditions, thankfully, but as we all know, it can be a drawn-out legal process that could take over ten years to settle in some cases and, even then, the winner would be unpredictable. The widow becomes homeless with her children and not his relatives, whose lives do not change at his passing.

Life in Glasgow

Julie left the island with the last child, who was starting university in Glasgow. She went back to the university to train as a social worker but had to drop out after a successful first year due to ill health. The trauma of the last three years had taken its toll more than Julie realised. After a while, she got a job as a carer and support worker as a quick fix because she was very unsettled and could not commit to fixed hours or full-time hours at any job. She was deciding whether to relocate to Nigeria, where she later spent the best part of the next few years putting things in place to that effect.

Julie liked socialising and had arrived in Glasgow without knowing anyone. She soon made good friends in church and joined the African and Caribbean Women's Association to make new friends, meet 'her people' and learn about Glasgow's social scene. The association, formed in 1988, brings together women from Africa, the Caribbean, and the diaspora, to meet the social, emotional, cultural, and educational needs of these women and their families. They did not disappoint as being part of this community organisation helped to settle Julie into the Glasgow social scene, and it is still a very relevant part of her life to this day. Julie became the organisation's Chair after nine years in Glasgow and successfully contributed to the organisation in that capacity for the next four years. Being a part of the organisation helps one keep in touch with one's roots, especially for the children coming behind the adults.

Julie was very proud to be part of the team that set up an African Children's Choir, which was very good for teaching the children self-confidence, self-acceptance and making new friends. Events like Black History Month and Africa Day gave them a chance also to proudly wear all the African clothes in the closet and celebrate their heritage. This organisation also celebrates Burns Night yearly with a ceilidh including Scottish, Asian, and African music and dancers with drums, bagpipes, and haggis! The organisation was a lifeline during the Covid-19 lockdown as members supported each other through weekly Zoom meetings, telephone calls and networking with other organisations for more support. The Zoom meetings helped a great deal to alleviate the feelings of isolation and despair during the lockdown.

Julie volunteers with other local and charitable community organisations both here and in Nigeria. Recently, she was appointed a Panel Member of Children's Hearing in Scotland. She hopes to use this opportunity to do what she loves best, caring for children and young people.

Her writing group in Glasgow was a life saver and a life changer. This group made Julie believe that she should never give up and that if one believes in writing, then keep at it and enjoy it as a hobby. There, Julie also learned that writing is very varied and that anyone can discover their niche. Some writers are best with fiction stories, romantic or crime, and others may be good at poetry, prose, or short pieces and reflections. Julie always wanted to write a story but got stuck on the wrong genre for years before discovering where her talent lay – in writing reflections and short pieces. This discovery was made possible by her engagement with the creative writing class. Julie enjoys being with this group of like-minded people. The gains are that one learns so much history, geography, science, etc., and one can also make good friends. They also go to book launches, book fairs and plays as a group.

Julie was at rock bottom, but she got up, recovered, and got on with her new 'single' life in a new city. She was reminded by her friend Osas of an old Benin adage which says, 'Aide gbera oto' which translates as, 'When you fall, you hit the ground. You cannot fall below the ground. The only other way is up.' Life is never more perfect than through hindsight. Julie beats herself up sometimes for not doing this or doing that, but in all that time, she was doing something possible and most important to her then. The lesson here is never to be too hard on yourself and the choices that you have made. There is always tomorrow for new adventures and misadventures!

Well, Julie chose to stay positive in her life and to appreciate what she was busy doing that was so important to her at any time. Take the example of the uncompleted PhD that she registered for and got to complete. It was a tribute to her late husband, who had typed all the original work and always felt guilty that she did not complete her PhD before dragging her off again when all she had left was the external defence. Julie was widowed at the time and found studying very therapeutic. She believed she would relocate to Nigeria at the time, so she spent a lot of time in Nigeria, but that never happened. Picking up her studies again was challenging because it was almost a brand-new thesis, except that the topic did not change. Doing it was very psychologically rewarding.

When she visited Nigeria, she met up with some of her original classmates, some of whom are now professors in their departments. The idea was to return to Nigeria for good and travel to the UK for visits. She spent years trying it out by living most of the year going backwards and forwards between the two countries; then the girls started having babies. In the end, Julie decided that living permanently in Nigeria was no longer an option. Her children and grandchildren were here in the UK, and she got lots of joy from helping the grandchildren while their parents went back to school for another full degree or furthered their employment.

Her five children have nine first degrees between them, some postgraduate degrees, and professional training. Julie has a first degree, a postgraduate diploma in Education, a Master's degree, and a PhD in Educational Psychology. Would she have it any other way? The answer is No. Julie would not change a thing. Life goes on with new exploits, interests, and discoveries.

Chapter 5

PRESIDENT BARACK OBAMA

Introduction

This essay is a result of reading Barack Obama's books and articles on Obama written by other authors, YouTube videos of his speeches, events, and news bulletins. I want to dedicate a part of my book to giving honour to President Obama. I contribute to this historical figure for the present and future generations who read my book. I wrote this chapter because I felt my book would not be complete without paying tribute to a man I consider a beacon of hope and light to this generation of young men and women. He has made the raising of our Black children a little bit easier. After all, we can point to him and say to them, 'Look at President Barack Obama. Work hard! Believe in yourself.'

Preamble

There have been many notable people and events that have happened in the last 100 years that have changed the way we look at the world one way or the other, especially from an ethnic minority point of view. We have notable Black icons like Martin Luther King, Rosa Parks, Nelson Mandela, Oprah Winfrey, Maya Angelou, Barack Obama, and many others, too numerous to name, who have contributed to the advancement of Black people all over the world. The freedom fighters, freedom writers and community organisers have helped shape the Black person's journey from slavery to being acknowledged as equal partners in humanity.

However, there are those fighting to maintain the status quo, keep Black people down, and maintain the 'white supremacy' lies by refusing to accept that all people are created equal. These racists come in all shapes and guises. The Black people's struggle in the world for equality indicates the status of Black people everywhere. Even on their own land, they were subjugated to being second-class citizens, their mineral resources plundered, and their leaders killed or imprisoned like Nelson Mandela, who spent 27 years in prison. The plunder and pillage of Africa are continuing in different trade and business guises, and the repercussions are still evident today.

We grew up with the mantra that America is the leader of the 'free' world and that whatever happens there reflects 'what is' and 'what should be'. So, it has been deplorable to watch from the outside the way some things have been, especially the recently much-publicised police brutality towards some Black people and the alleged mass incarceration of Black men on alleged minor and bogus charges to fill up the commercial jail houses. As Martin Luther King wrote in his letter from the city jail of Birmingham, Alabama, on 16 April 1963,

> Injustice anywhere is a threat to justice everywhere. We are caught in an inescapable network of mutuality, tied in a single garment of destiny. Whatever affects one directly, affects all indirectly.[4]

Anti-racist movements march in peaceful protests to demand equality, respect and dignity from the police and the justice system, with very little progress achieved. This lack of sufficient progress reflects the discrimination and disadvantage suffered by Black people in the Western world in all spheres of life against this backdrop of lynchings, police brutality and mass incarcerations. We hear all this about America and other places, yet that does not diminish America as a land of opportunity where 'anyone' can be what they are capable of being when the opportunity arises. America is a melting pot though the Black struggle remains a real problem even today. Black people may sometimes work twice as hard or have more mitigating circumstances to climb the ladder, making it even more remarkable when Black people achieve spectacular successes against all odds.

We could name many icons of the twenty-first century, but who stands out for me is Barack Obama because of

---

[4] Martin Luther King Jr, 'Letter from a Birmingham Jail [King, Jr]' (16 April 1963), African Studies Center – University Of Pennsylvania: https://www.africa.upenn.edu/Articles_Gen/Letter_Birmingham.html (accessed: 26 March 2021).

the confidence, foresight, self-belief, and intelligence that brought about the first Black president of the United States of America. His book, *The Audacity of Hope*, and his use of the slogan 'Yes we can!' reflect the optimism we felt for ourselves and our children, who felt liberated and were walking around with pride. Here comes hope, peace, love, brilliance, strength, resilience, compassion, truth, faithfulness, loyalty and pride, all embodied in one man. Whenever I think about hope and change, only one person comes to mind, Barack Obama. It is still a wonder that a Black man surmounted all those obstacles, prejudices, hatred and discrimination to emerge as the 44th President of the United States of America, the most powerful nation on earth. How did he do it? How did he achieve this lofty height? He did it for all Black children, mixed-race children, ethnic minority people, and Black or white people from single-parent households or non-privileged backgrounds, very educated people who value knowledge and all who value meritocracy above cronyism. Julie became fascinated by this man.

She repeatedly asked herself, 'How did he transcend all the obstacles to triumph so spectacularly?' America is indeed a land of milk and honey, a melting pot, and one can dare to dream and accomplish one's goals in America more than in any other country in the world. Many alive today never imagined that they would live to see the day that a Black man was sworn in as an American President. No one could have predicted that there would be a Black president with a Black wife in the White House in their generation or the next generation, and how he comported himself with grace!

Politics

I first became aware of Barack Obama during the democratic primaries that he contested with Hillary Clinton. I was immediately drawn to him, and everything reported about him. I wondered then, 'Who is this Black man whose oratory can electrify an audience?' I listened to all the debates he had with Hillary Clinton, and I still was not hopeful but glad that he had even got that far. It seemed inconceivable that America was ready for a Black president. I then searched his name and found the keynote address he gave in 2004 at the Democratic National Convention in Boston, Massachusetts, which has since been dubbed 'The speech that made Obama President' by the media. I was riveted to my seat while listening to that speech on a YouTube video. It was simply electrifying, and I had great respect for the man because I knew that much preparation had gone into that speech. He had the intelligence and ability to deliver it with effect.

I have listened to that speech many times over the years. I was so inspired and moved by Barack's speeches that I have read and listened to his speeches at various times. I admire Obama's charisma and confidence.

Obama's Election Victory Speech in 2008 was another captivating speech delivered after the euphoria of his election win.

His books

Obama is a prolific writer with many books to his name. Below are the titles of some of his books.

- *Dreams from My Father*
- *The Audacity of Hope*
- *Of Thee I Sing: A Letter to My Daughters*
- *Change We Can Believe In*
- *A Promised Land.*

Family man: His rock, Michelle

Barack and Michelle met at the Sidley law firm in Chicago, where she was an attorney, and he worked as a summer associate while enrolled in law school. They were married on 3 October 1992. They have two daughters, Malia, born on 4 July 1998, and Natasha (known as Sasha), born on 10 July 2001. Talking about his children, Obama told Essence.com,

'The great thing about the girls is that they have got a wonderful role model in their mom. They've seen how Michelle and I interact – not only the love but also the respect that I show to their mum.'[5]

The love story of Barack Obama and Michelle Obama is endearing for all to see.

The adage that behind every successful man is a strong woman could not be truer for this powerful couple. Michelle is the author of the book *Becoming*. Michelle is a notable role model for girls, especially Black girls

---

[5] L. Porter, 'All Of The Times Barack Obama Professed His Love For The First Lady' (26 October 2020), Essence.com: https://www.essence.com/celebrity/black-celeb-couples/best-barack-obama-quotes-michelle-obama/#81869 (accessed: October 2021).

worldwide. She tells them it is cool to be studious and hardworking and has lived it for all to see.

Legacy

Barack's agent told him to change his name to Barry, but he refused because he was proud of his African heritage. He brought his family from Kenya to his inauguration in the United States. What a gesture, demonstrating pride in his African heritage and signalling to the world that all people are created equal, and we are all important, irrespective of socio-economic status. Obama practises what he preaches: Americans and the world are one people, irrespective of colour, race, or language.

Barack Obama was awarded the Nobel Peace Prize in October 2009 for his 'extraordinary efforts to strengthen international diplomacy and cooperation between peoples'.[6] He was also a recipient of many other awards. Political commentators may question some aspects of his accomplishments during his tenure, as he could not accomplish all he wanted, due to the political system's functioning. However, his legacy to all well-meaning Americans, African Americans, and Black people worldwide is an outstanding accomplishment with the economy and other legislative successes. It is not in the scope of this essay to go into his political achievements but suffice it to say that he won two terms in office, the administration was scandal-free, and the rest is politics.

---

[6] Britannica, 'Barack Obama: Facts & Related Content': https://www.britannica.com/facts/Barack-Obama (accessed: 29 June 2022).

He will forever be in history as the first African American President of the United States of America.

His attempts to change things proved difficult sometimes because of politics, such as gun control. Gun control remains a big problem in America, even past President Obama's regime. He did not come from a privileged background and could transcend all obstacles, prejudices, and stereotyping to prevail. He urged young people to 'reject pessimism and cynicism' and 'know that progress is possible, and problems can be solved'.[7]

Barack Obama is a role model, professor, lawyer, lecturer, community organiser, published author, orator, good family man, sincere and compassionate, humorous, and a pioneer who achieved all these things without any privileges. I have watched his many speeches, and there is always humour. He was also a singing and dancing president. He delivered the eulogy at the service for the church leader and South Carolina State Senator Clementa Pinckney, who was among nine people shot dead in Charleston. Obama's 'Amazing Grace' will be remembered for a long time. He led the singing of 'Amazing Grace' during the eulogy, which was very poignant, uplifting, and meaningful and a great comfort to everyone in that congregation and beyond. His empathy was genuine and heartfelt. He never stopped relating to his roots and his people, even in the

---

[7] BBC News, 'President Obama tells young to reject cynicism' (23 April 2016): https://www.bbc.co.uk/news/uk-36119829 (accessed: 1 September 2022).

highest office. Also, I still watch Obama dancing during the musical shows at the White House.

Conclusion

Post-presidency, Obama remains an influential figure in American life and a role model to all well-wishers worldwide. He is an icon of the twenty-first century, and there is no better time than now to demonstrate the culmination of Black life struggles with his success and promote fair play and equality for all races.

As a grandmother to eleven grandchildren, nine boys and two girls, Obama (and Michelle) will forever remain a song on our familiy's lips. He may be a different generation from some Black activists like Martin Luther King, some of whom shed blood to pave the way for this new generation. Obama's impact has raised the aspiration of a whole new generation of young boys and girls and made everything a little more accessible. Anytime my 14-year-old grandson is being lazy, makes excuses, or blames somebody else for bad behaviour, our family weapon is always to use the name of Obama. It is a name that resonates with kids all over the world. It has helped them to see what is possible and to never give in to detractors, racists, or cynicism. Instead, the best way to fight negativity is to achieve success against all odds. The path may be rough, but belief in oneself, hard work, diligence, resilience, positivity, hope and determination will triumph over adversity, racism, discrimination, underestimation and so on.

Obama is a culmination of what the civil rights movement fought for: the opportunity for Black people to show their abilities and capabilities with or without oppression. Obama did this through his ability to overcome all the prejudices and obstacles on the way. He stood tall and said: 'Yes, we can.'

Questions for grandchildren:

Who was the first Black President of America?

Did anyone see it coming? If not, why?

What skin colour is his wife, Michelle?

When he was growing up, was he 'rich'?

So, how did he do it? (This is the big question for discussion with our children.)

Many everyday achievers are great role models for our children: teachers, doctors, nurses, engineers, scientists, firefighters, soldiers, politicians, business people, fathers, and mothers. They are all heroes and heroines. Obama is a modern-day icon of his generation, an embodiment of all that is excellent, unique, pioneering, gracious, sound, and admirable. He is known to everyone worldwide for his good deeds and he is a Black man.

One child asked the other, 'Why are you black?'

The child replied, 'I don't know!' and asked, 'Why are you white?'

The other child replied, 'I don't know!'

Patricia Iredia

The Journey Continues

Chapter 6

THE LEGACY OF SLAVERY

Julie watched a BBC *Question Time* programme where an 'aggressive' panellist voiced a solid anti-immigrant position. When tackled by the audience, she noticed how cleverly he said, 'I agree with you, but …' several times to calm down the irate responders. As a politician worried about the audience's approval, he articulated his party's position on racial issues.

It may be assumed that all parties stand for the same values to a great extent, which is 'making Britain great' from different perspectives and 'modus operandi'. Even though the lines between the main parties have blurred over the years, particularly about business, economy, education, immigration and so on, the same cannot be said for some 'nationalist' parties, which are openly and divisively anti-immigrant and appear to be set up for that purpose. Having said this, we would like to believe that the whole point of debates and elections is to find a candidate that can deliver the mandate, irrespective of style or beliefs. It does not matter what party one belongs to, what manifesto promises are presented, the immigrant rhetoric, or how colourful the leader's personality is. What matters is getting the job done for the good of the nation.

Brexit

The issue of Brexit has dominated our psyches for the past six years as everyone slowly comes to terms with the reality and how it impacts them and their generation. In a referendum held on 23 June 2016, many Britons, almost 51.9% of those voting, voted to leave the European Union (EU), which the UK had joined in 1973, and 48.1% voted to remain.[8] How did we get here? In 2015, the Conservative General Election victory pledged to hold an in-out referendum on the UK's membership of the EU. David Cameron had made the promise during the campaign along party lines. Unfortunately, he lost the vote, and the Leave campaign won by 51.9% to 48.1%. Cameron was a Remainer.

In March 2017, the countdown to the UK formally leaving the EU, also known as 'Brexit', began. Many people like this author did not digest all the arguments for or against at the time. Instead, many people were already entrenched in their beliefs which in turn informed their

---

[8] UK Parliament, Research Briefing: 'Analysis of the EU Referendum results 2016' (29 June 2016), House of Commons Library: https://commonslibrary.parliament.uk/research-briefings/cbp-7639/ (accessed: 28 February 2022).

rigid stance. Opinions were very strong on both sides of the debate. Still, it is refreshing to note that, for an issue as important as Brexit, politicians and members of the public were divided evenly within parties and families. It has been difficult to find a consensus as the topic is complex and has serious ramifications for polity and the populace from different backgrounds.

When the result of the referendum was announced, Julie, like so many across the world, was astounded. She was far away in Africa at the time and sadly missed out on voting. She felt a deep sense of guilt that she did not exercise her moral and civic obligation to vote, even though one vote would not have made a difference to the result of the referendum. The referendum may have been lost by many Remainers being complacent on voting day, so every vote counts is a lesson for all. She can still remember her physical reaction to the news, which was a piercing scream of 'Oh no! My God, where were you?'

She questioned God, asking, 'Why did you allow this to happen?' From a Remainer's point of view, it was like a bereavement for Julie.

'Why would I want to be confined to one corner of the continent when I can be a citizen of the whole of Europe?' As one immigrant said, 'Did I flee my country, suffer to become a European citizen to end up being confined to the UK? I now need a "visa" to the rest of Europe. What about my children and grandchildren who live there?' Julie's cousin, Kate is particularly pained because she had the option to remain in Italy but chose to put down roots in the UK because of her husband's job. They could have stayed in Italy. Instead, the family is scattered worldwide. Kate's relatives, including their mother, now live in Italy with their oldest sibling after their father's passing. Just like Julie, Katee emigrated to Europe from Africa in the early eighties. . Shee had thought, 'Travel between EU countries is easy. I can join my family in Italy after retirement.'

No one predicted that one day Britain would withdraw from the EU. Kate's story is just one human story that is a consequence of Britain's 'divorce' from Europe.

People had got so used to being citizens of Europe that the alternative seemed inconceivable. The advantages of freedom of movement, liberty to live, be educated and work in Europe for British citizens are gone. There is now a scramble for European passports by British citizens via family connections in European countries. There is the story of another Black woman born in Belfast, Northern Ireland, who applied for and got an Irish passport, encouraged by her white friends who were doing the same. To use her own words, 'It is my entitlement, and I am doing it for my children and grandchildren; their colour already disadvantages them, so it is better to have more choices and more opportunities open to them.' Those in the ethnic minority group do not know how all this will play out in the long run. People are reacting to the fear of being 'boxed in' and marginalised.

Brexit has been a wake-up call for some racists to let loose on the immigrants. The statistics on racist attacks show that there has been an increase since the referendum. Robert Booth stated that:

> Ethnic minorities in Britain are facing rising and increasingly overt racism with levels of abuse and

discrimination continuing to grow in the wake of the Brexit referendum, nationwide research reveals.

Seventy-one per cent of people from ethnic minorities now report having faced racial discrimination, compared with 58% in January 2016, before the EU vote, according to polling data seen by the Guardian.[9]

Whatever the good intentions of Brexiteers were, one clear message they seem to have succeeded in sending to people was that immigrants are not welcome in this country. Documentary evidence, as stated above, suggests that racist attacks have increased since the announcement of the referendum results. An African woman who has been living in this country for 40 years said that she was shocked when debris was thrown at her on the street by two young white boys as she went to the corner shop for some groceries. They shouted, 'Go back to your own country.'

She replied, 'This is my country, too; I will die here.'

To which they mimicked monkey sounds. Racism used to be subtle, sometimes just the look one got, but now the racists have become more overt in their abuse and even carry out physical attacks.

---

[9] R. Booth, 'Racism rising since Brexit vote, nationwide study reveals', *The Guardian* (20 May 2019): https://www.theguardian.com/world/2019/may/20/racism-on-the-rise-since-brexit-vote-nationwide-study-reveals (accessed: 21 October 2020).

No one is wholly dismissing all the arguments for Brexit, but ordinary folk on the street do not go into the details of what microeconomics or macroeconomics are, or how they affect the economy, monetary union, or the high political spectrum, the struggle for dominance in Europe, the fear of being eclipsed as a sovereign nation, and so on. Ordinary folk do not grapple with that; that is left to the politicians to handle and simplify for us. So, were the populace told the truth about why the UK wanted to exit the EU? Were the campaign pledges about the NHS getting £350 million extra every week correct? Were the immigration permutations correct? Politicians have a moral and civic responsibility not to mislead the public.

Were their scare stories of 'Remain' outcomes correct?

Were the lofty promises of a Brexit outcome realistic or even truthful?

Were the Remainers' fears justified?

This author is particularly concerned about the effect of Brexit on racism. Some voters voted to leave because they disliked foreigners living and working in their country. They did not think of the interchange in the system, the isolation from Europe, the loss of skilled labour or even seasonal workers. This group abhor immigrants, especially those of a different colour. What do they want to happen to the immigrant population already in this country? Some have lived here their entire adult lives or arrived as children. Some people of colour were born here, and some families have lived here for generations.

Some reasons for ignorant racist behaviour towards Black people could be attributed to the absence of Black contributions to history in the curriculum. Including Black contributions throughout world history will educate the populace on: why immigrants are here, what history they share with this country as Commonwealth citizens, what sacrifices they have made for this country, and the consequences of unwillingness by some people to accept others as equal human beings. When one explores this country's history of colonisation throughout the Commonwealth, the demonisation of foreigners should not be tolerated or encouraged by any side of the debate. The focus can be on other parameters like sovereignty or economic gains, but not on immigrants being blamed for societal ills and accused of taking jobs.

No one could have predicted the disproportionate impact on Black frontline workers when the Covid -19 pandemic started. The first reported deaths of National Health Service (NHS) workers were mostly of immigrants who were doctors, nurses, cleaners and security guards, taxi drivers, bus drivers, and others in frontline jobs. Black, Asian, and Minority Ethnic (BAME) workers paid the ultimate price with their lives in the wake of the coronavirus for various reasons such as poverty and the nature of the jobs they do as frontline workers: security, bus drivers, taxi drivers, and carers. Immigrants are often accused of taking the jobs of local people when they want to work and support their families.

The poverty and ills of society affect Black people differently and most adversely because of their socio-economic situation and being frontline workers. Loss of jobs and having no recourse to public funds has thrown some asylum seekers into poverty. Most immigrants have not come here to collect benefits and be liabilities.

The majority are honest, hardworking people. Very few immigrants are criminals as in any other groups.

If polls are to be believed, everyone may have lost out due to the short-sightedness of some politicians and the lies they told to win the referendum. Every former prime minister from both parties was a Remainer. Listening to those who were on the world stage and had the unique advantage of understanding all the arguments should have meant something. Unfortunately, the armchair generals propagating political inexactitudes and political contradictions, with less experience in world politics, surmised that Brexit was best for the UK. Some of them were probably playing the immigration card for their own political and economic gain, not for the collective good of the country.

When discussing Brexit, for instance, immigrants are by no means a homogenous group. They are found on both sides of the political debate and are divided for various reasons, including selfishness. One example cited from an anonymous post that was going around before the referendum by an irate African doctor made sense to him at the time because he felt he was negatively affected by discrimination. He claimed that European doctors were getting the jobs and being provided with interpreters at a high cost to the NHS, while Black doctors from English-speaking countries already here were starting to find it hard to get jobs. He was advocating that Black immigrants should vote for Brexit. Apart from personal issues (some may call it selfish), as in this example, most immigrants remember that they were immigrants themselves and that everyone deserves to be treated with dignity, respect, fairness and equality, whether you can speak perfect English or not. However, this is far from the reality mentioned above, especially for Black people with a unique history of slavery, racism and discrimination.

Migration

The legacy of slavery and its impact on people's consciousness is real. Racism affects everyone who is a foreigner to varying degrees; it does not matter how long one has been in this country or even if one was born here; racists make assumptions about immigrants. It is sometimes assumed that foreigners are here to collect welfare benefits, but this assumption is very far from reality. Most came to build train lines or work in other fields. The history of why foreigners, like the Windrush generation, came to this country is a legacy of colonisation, which is another topic for discussion. Uprooting from one's own country and coming to the UK is not a decision that anyone makes lightly. There are myriad reasons for the recent inflow of refugees from all over the world. Some are obvious: war-torn zones, persecuted people, and displaced people who have lost everything and came here to seek asylum. Some others are not asylum seekers or refugees but immigrants who have come here to join spouses and family for education or business.

This new wave of immigrants unfolding on land, sea, and air smacks of desperation. We have watched documentaries of Africans in Libya trying to cross into Europe. Many small boats capsized, and the bodies were washed ashore along the beach. The asylum seekers looked on in horror at the spectacle while women wailed, having recognised some of the deceased. Yet, they were ready to set sail on the next dinghy.

The arrival of asylum seekers on these shores is not a new phenomenon. The UK welcomed various war refugees in the past, like some from 'Biafra' during the Nigerian Civil War. What seems to be different now is the spectacle of the mass movement of refugees, men, women, and children, seen on boats and dinghies willing to risk their lives to reach safety in Europe. Some refugees would be bogus or miscreants, but the sea of humanity moving *en masse* in all directions fleeing the carnage empty-handed, having left everything behind, was real.

Many new arrivals were from non-English speaking countries, so locals complained of pressure on local services: schools, hospitals and housing. Locals have a point if affected by the lack of adequate provisions to meet needs in the community because of the influx of refugees. The government can and should provide adequate services to meet the needs of its citizens. The UK is a rich country that can afford to help when there is a global crisis to which a global response is needed. It is a basic human need to seek safety and refuge, and the United Nations Declaration of Human Rights applies to everybody equally.

Discrimination does not affect only recent refugees or asylum seekers; it affects ethnic minority people, regardless of how long they have lived in the UK. Even when born here and having lived here all their lives, ethnic minorities still experience discrimination at all levels. Their children must frequently answer this teacher's question: 'Did you do this by yourself, or did your parent do it for you?'

They may be marked down because some teachers refuse to accept their ability. They mostly work twice as hard as their white mates to prove themselves. The job market is another big hurdle to jump over, and their treatment on the job is the same, with various obstacles in the way of inclusion and promotion. They are generally never good enough for that managerial post. Black kids are bullied by their peers, teachers, the police, the justice system, and society. This prejudice leaves frustrated, confused children who are consequently labelled aggressive and angry. On record, they suffer more mental health issues than their peers and are above the general population's average, especially compared to children in Africa.

Everyone is supposed to know their place, whatever that means to the individual. The message society is teaching Black children about themselves is summed up in the phrase, 'Who do you think you are?' There seem to be no allowances made for differences in temperament, character, ability, motivation, etc. Are they all supposed to be clones of one another? They may be timid, subservient, lacking confidence, and staying poor, and yet this cannot guarantee their safety when stopped by the police. We have seen videos and reports from the other side of the Atlantic, all the 'accidental' deaths at routine traffic stops and the shooting of some Black men even when their backs were turned and they were running away. It might not be so common here in the UK, but some cases have been reported of police profiling and brutality towards Black people.

We have seen video clips of 14-year-old boys mistreated and handcuffed while their white friends looked on. When one considers the stories of some Black people and their experiences with police, teachers in the classroom, peers, co-workers, offices and even shops where they are sometimes followed around like prospective shoplifters, racism is confirmed.

On the way to the bus station to catch an overnight bus to London for a funeral, the police stopped Julie's son with her in the car. He was 18 years old and a university student at the time. There was no traffic violation, and he was not told why he was stopped. He was told to step out of the car and asked, 'What have you got in your car?'

He answered, 'Nothing.'

Two policemen stood very close to him with their bodies touching him and their hands folded across their chests, squared up to him as if he was a criminal. He was then subjected to a very humiliating and aggressive body search, and they searched his car inside and outside.

One of the police officers even lay on the ground to inspect the car's tyres meticulously, before stamping his licence with three points for a loose thread on one tyre! The garage told him the next day that the tyre was not sufficiently damaged to warrant points on his licence. It was not due for a change, but he changed it anyway for fear of encountering the same team again. That was the second time he had been stopped that week, and none of his white friends had ever experienced that. He lost his trust in the police that day and, most importantly, his innocence about equality for all.

Windrush

It is easy to relate the biased aspect of Brexit with what we have seen happening with the Windrush generation, where generations of people who have lived in the UK since childhood were denied citizenship and secretly deported from the country. Their parents were invited to come to the 'motherland' to help rebuild the country, 'Your country needs you' was printed on flyers. Can people be wished away for flimsy excuses even though they were born here, lived here, and worked here before any detrimental retrospective immigration laws came into effect? It is like someone was looking for an excuse to expel immigrants.

The Windrush generation was treated as though they had no rights or legal standing; people were subjected to scrutiny and standards that were difficult to defend and uphold morally. How can a teenage misdemeanour disqualify a grown man or woman from citizenship when he or she is now on the straight and narrow, has a job, pays his or her taxes, has a partner and children? The Windrush community had their share of miscreants, like all other communities in the UK. This law appears to attempt to disenfranchise many people in marginalised groups. Surely, there is more to a man than one non-violent indiscretion as a child or teenager? Are we, as a society, looking for any excuse to demonise the immigrants and deprive them of their legitimate human rights of equality?

Jamie Grierson,[10] on the Windrush scandal, reported on the scheme that began refusing people deemed ineligible for citizenship for failure to meet good character requirements. The Government Report on the Windrush scandal agreed that racism was involved in making negative decisions. The Home Secretary, Priti Patel, said 'work is continuing' to ensure 'those who suffered receive the documentation and compensation they need'.[11] This gesture came too late for many victims.

Racial profiling

What happened to George Floyd on 25 May 2020, in Minneapolis, Minnesota, USA, brought home to many the way Black people continue to be treated: the value of the lives of Black people. The image of Derek Chauvin's knee on George Floyd's neck for 9 minutes 29 seconds, or 8 minutes 46 seconds as first thought, while he slowly lynched him to death in full public view testified to the suffering of Black people at the hands of the police everywhere, especially in America. The image sent shock waves through every decent human being worldwide, causing protests against police brutality,

---

[10] J. Grierson, 'Windrush scandal: UK's Windrush scheme begins refusing people deemed ineligible for citizenship' (21 September 2018), *The Guardian*: https://www.theguardian.com/uk-news/2018/sep/21/uk-windrush-scheme-begins-refusing-people-ineligible-for-citizenship (accessed:10 January 2021).

[11] UK Parliament, 'Priti Patel makes statement on Windrush compensation scheme' (23 June 2020): https://www.parliament.uk/business/news/2020/june/windrush-statement/ (accessed 10 January 2021).

especially towards Black people, quickly spreading across the United States and internationally.

Policing in the UK may not have such a graphic incident, and the racism might not be so blatant and rampant, but racial profiling, harassment, and alleged murder or manslaughter of some Black people by police are also documented here as in the US. The case of Sheku Bayoh is an ongoing case of another death in police custody in the UK. 'It is less than five minutes since the police arrived, and Sheku Bayoh is dying on the pavement with his hands and legs bound. He never gets back up ...'[12] It often plays out in public for all to see the different approaches to policing Black and white people: Blacks are treated with disrespect and brutality, while their white counterparts are treated with respect and kid gloves. There is no hiding place for Black people; a simple traffic stop by the police can escalate to become deadly, as has been reported many times across the Atlantic.

These exaggerations of Black crime, racial profiling and violence towards Black people, have led to many lives being taken with careless disregard for the sanctity of life. They are swift to put points on their driver's licences, drag them through the courts with bogus charges, and the courts play their part by issuing heavier sentences on Black people. Sometimes, it is like a deliberate attempt to criminalise many young Black men to disadvantage them in their life opportunities. It is well known that a

---

[12] M. Daly and C. McKay, 'Sheku Bayoh: 'Why did my brother die in police custody' (18 January 2021), *BBC News*. Updated: https://www.bbc.co.uk/news/uk-scotland-53076269 (accessed: 18 June 2022).

simple 'Yes' or 'No' answer to the question 'Have you ever been arrested by the police?' has far-reaching implications for the lives of those who answer 'Yes'. So how can it be fair that some sections of the community are unfairly targeted, stereotyped, arrested, and slammed for minor offences or no offence other than a resemblance to someone the police are looking for? This targeting has an impact on their job opportunities and even travel opportunities when seeking to obtain visas. This police behaviour seriously impacts the health and well-being of our immigrant community. It must be stressed that it is not every policeman or woman that acts in a racist manner, but some do, which is one too many with dire consequences for the victims.

People from Black, Asian, and Minority Ethnic (BAME) backgrounds are over-represented in our prison population. David Lammy states that the treatment of BAME groups in the criminal justice system has got 'considerably worse' since his review.[13]

The impact of police brutality is felt wherever it occurs all over the world, but the difference with racism as a factor in arrests is that one is targeted just for the colour of one's skin. Recently, there have been 'End Special Anti-Robbery Squad' (End SARS) demonstrations in Nigeria. It was an exposition of police oppression of the powerless who are traumatised by these encounters.

---

[13] M. Bulman, Independent, 'David Lammy says treatment of BAME groups in criminal justice system has got "considerably worse" since his review' (26 March 2019), *The Independent* :
https://www.independent.co.uk/news/uk/home-news/david-lammy-review-bame-criminal-justice-black-ethnic-minority-a8840306.html
(accessed: 10 January 2022.

The effect on the psyche and well-being is similar but not quite the same, as in the West it is sometimes based on skin colour, whilst in Africa it is based on economics.

'End SARS' was a decentralised social movement of mass protests against police brutality in Nigeria. The slogan called for the disbanding of the 'Special Anti-Robbery Squad (SARS)', a notorious unit of the Nigerian police with an alleged long record of abuse, killings, assaults and harassment. This particular police unit in Nigeria was allegedly using its position to corruptly exploit the masses by extorting money from everyone they could catch on bogus charges. No young person was safe from them; if one had a beautiful car, one became a target for extortion. The police were also accused of being brutal when they could not get money from people. The leaders of the 'End SARS' movement came from every sector and every region of Nigeria.

Every citizen felt the same pain, but racism in policing is different and worse because brutality and high-handedness are sometimes selective against people in the Black community. Mostly, there are no consequences for attacks on Black people, as police sometimes bungle investigations because they do not care about the victims of racist crime, as happened in the Stephen Lawrence case, which was later characterised in the Macpherson report as 'institutional racism'. The Black African is at the bottom of the rung. They are constantly being disproportionately targeted, humiliated, stopped, handcuffed and dehumanised by the police and the legal system.

For most Nigerians living in the UK, most of our families abroad see us as being like our white counterparts,

British citizens who have spent most of our adult lives in our adopted country. All our children were born here. Paradoxically, some treat us as foreigners in the UK, and all the rhetoric from some sectors is to make one feel like a second-class citizen. The result is that discrimination results in policies like the Windrush legislation that undermine many British ethnic minorities here to feel like they do not belong.

Raising Black children

Parents face many challenges while raising Black children in a white environment against the backdrop of discrimination, oppression and injustices. The problem within the Black community is how to raise Black children to live within societal norms without being singled out by the police, teachers and others in authority. Especially, when it is evident that their white friends do not get lectures from their parents on how to behave around the police and elsewhere to survive the system. Black children are intentionally or unintentionally taught to tolerate insults and jibes to avoid frequent confrontations with others.

The norms are interpreted differently for Black children and their white mates; 'work hard' takes on a different meaning if one is Black. It means 'work doubly hard; you have no privileges which can give you leverage and the benefit of the doubt'. For instance, how would you explain to a Black child not to run too fast so that he does not win and offend the locals? This happened to an immigrant family that moved into a new community. One of their five children was good at sport and, on sports day, came top in some events in primary school. Her neighbour, who was watching the sports with them, whispered to the child's mother, 'The local children have always won these titles, so they may not be too happy.'

Should the Black parent have said to her child, 'Please do not run too fast, so you do not win and offend the locals?'

Shouldn't kids be kids? Obviously, 'No', not some, not when they are Black. Must they be defined by their colour, social origin, and a stereotype rather than their character or skills?

No matter how clever Black kids are, they may suffer in the school system. They struggle so much for acceptance from peers that they are sometimes socially and psychologically messed up. How do you console a child who gets the best possible result in her final examinations with perfect high scores across all subjects and all elements of every subject, but comes home looking depressed, due to rejection by peers? She said, 'Something funny happened today.'

'What was it?' her mum asked.

'As I ran towards my mates, they all ran away from me giggling,' she replied.

How does one console such a child? How do you explain that she has to keep trying to belong and make excuses for others when it is such a herculean task to belong, especially if you are from an ethnic minority and very clever at school?

Attention must be paid to the mental health of ethnic minority children, so it is not enough to be very clever at school; they need to have a sense of belonging, to make friends and have a safe and stable home for support. Parents must provide a stable home for their children to empower them to face the world confidently.

Change is possible

The ethnic minority people who are here are here to stay. This country is their home too. Some were born here and know nothing else than being citizens of this great country. Having noted the discrimination that Black people and other ethnic minorities face daily does not exclude the fact that some have 'succeeded' against this backdrop; not every person in authority is racist or biased or discriminates against them. Black or ethnic minority people have shown resilience and strength to remain engaged with the polity of their communities. With all the debates going on about racism and how to tackle the associated issues, there is room for optimism that change is possible. It is a long time coming, but it is coming.

Every human being is a politician to varying degrees. Who does not care about the issues that plague everyday living, that define our standard of living? Who would not care about their children's education or the healthcare system, the state of the economy, and how it impacts their lives? In all spheres of life, we must be different to some degree to bring different experiences, ideas, skills and opinions to the table. It is essential to express one's view and be able to do so within reasonable ethical and moral limits. That's the difference between a fascist government and a democratic one. In the latter, everyone can join the debate.

People may or may not agree with you on everything you stand for, but might also leave having learnt something new, be it a way of seeing the world or a jolt to reality. We cannot be clones of one another. Someone else will always have something new to bring to the table. Someone else can achieve the same goals with a very different style. The beauty of changing leaders while the machinery or the principles of government don't change radically is the different approaches. Who has not watched an episode of *Yes, Minister* and seen Sir Humphrey's antics with the hapless Minister, Jim Hacker, all in the attempt to keep the machinery of government running without changes? But it does change, albeit slowly.

Believing that you can do anything you set your mind on is vital. There's always room to learn from past and present, evolve, and contribute to the ongoing debate or task. Who would have thought that, one day, Scotland would have its first immigrant African and Caribbean councillors elected in 2017? It took lots of guts to believe they could do it and go for it. Their election shows that attitudes are not stagnant and that an individual's opinion of another's capability based on whatever premise is not a consensus and can be very wrong and myopic. The most important thing is for Black men and women to have the freedom to pursue their dreams. To have the free will to decide for themselves what is best for them, to know their abilities and opportunities and to exercise that inalienable right of freedom of choice and expression as others.

The immigration question is by no means the only topic that brings out the issues of 'fear of change' to what we perceive to be 'normal': people change, history changes, leaders come and go, some leaving us with the notion that our differences are insurmountable, and the only way is to go back in time and separate the human race back to their pre-exploration and pre-colonial times and before the building of ships, aeroplanes, radio and the internet. It is pertinent to emancipate oneself from dogma, feel free, see the good and the potential in others, and move on without being bogged down by the 'fear of change.' Fear of change is also a factor for immigrants who cite every unpleasant past action by others as discriminatory.

Whether in love, friendship or politics on a global stage or the fringes, one thing is definite to be happy or successful in life – free yourself from mental slavery: do not be afraid to express your opinion, to follow your dreams, to believe in yourself, to learn and change and to make your impact on the world or your corner of it.

The most painful part of this saga for families was being torn apart by war.

Patricia Iredia

The Journey Continues

Chapter 7

THE WARS AND MORE

Many incidents from her childhood can still make Julie shudder, but nothing compares to what she witnessed as a child while she was visiting her grandparents. She liked visiting her grandma because she relished the opportunity of a few pennies from her grandma for Cadbury's chocolate from the newly opened supermarket on the main street near Grandma's place. Both the supermarket and chocolates were novelties as the chocolate was a change from the hard colourful sweets she usually had at home. Those coloured candies were guaranteed to peel the roof of your mouth after licking one sweet, so eating a bar of Cadbury's chocolate was lush.

Grandma was a small-scale businesswoman selling live goats from farms in the market to retailers and restaurants and was a very generous person, especially as Julie's mum was her only surviving child who bore her 11 of the 13 grandchildren she had. Grandma lived in the oldest part of Benin City, in the centre of town on the main street near the Catholic Cathedral, while Julie lived in the newer part of town called 'New Benin' with her parents, and in those days, a journey of one and a half miles between both houses was walking distance for children. Grandma's house was a harem, as Julie's polygamous grandad had at least three wives in the home at any time. Some young wives came and went, leaving their young children behind for the remaining wives.

The wives got younger as time passed, and they came and left. The only stable ones were the two oldest wives, of which Julie's grandma was the oldest and the first. She never left. Julie's mum was the oldest of her four children, two of whom did not survive childhood ailments in those days, and the third sibling passed at childbirth, leaving two children behind.

The contrast between Julie's house and her grandpa's house was stark. Julie's home was a monogamous household with her father and mother only. The children were not even allowed to venture out of the compound into a neighbour's house; street food from hawkers was not an option. In Grandpa's house, one could have hot and peppery rice wrapped in green leaves for breakfast bought from a street vendor. One could always go to Grandma and Grandpa to demand money for snacks and treats. There were lots of street food and lots of children to play games with; all this made Grandma's house very attractive to visit, and Julie and her siblings all clamoured to go there for the weekend. In fact, you had to be of good behaviour for the whole week to be allowed a weekend away with Grandma during the school holidays. Visits were continuously rotated during holidays as a different child was magically the better behaved as each week went by, and poor Grandma was constantly on the lookout for her grandchildren to stop them from straying out of sight while visiting her.

The Nigerian Civil War

Summer 1967 was a memorable time for Julie when she visited her grandma. At the start of the Biafran War in Nigeria, Julie was 11 years old and in the first year of secondary school at a Catholic boarding school which was an hour away from home, and she had to return home in a hurry. What were the chances in a lifetime of being caught up in the middle of a war? It all started as a political issue before the young Julie became caught up in it.

Life was going on every day as usual for Julie. Back in Africa, we heard of discrimination based on ethnic background, not colour. The discrimination and nepotism there were directed at which area of the country you came from; for instance, are you a northerner, westerner, easterner or southerner? What language do you speak? One was firmly identified by what religion one proclaimed. As they were growing up, everyone lived very peacefully together, celebrated each other's ceremonies, attended integrated schools and boarding schools, ate together, and shopped in the same market. It did not matter what part of town one came from. One's friends' list had on it both Christian and Muslim names and all tribes, and there was no difference in your mind. There were intermarriages among all tribes, including Christians and Muslims, and there was mutual respect for each other's religion. Julie grew up in childlike trust and innocence of all the political nuances that occurred.

Life was not as rosy as this perfect picture painted by a child's eye. There were a lot of political and religious undercurrents brewing all the time, right from the very first republic when the British put Northern and Southern protectorates together in 1914 to form Nigeria into one country. The North was predominantly Muslim and the South Christian, so there has always been a power struggle. The North was aided by the British to be dominant from the start, even though they were less educated at the time. While the politicians were screwing us up, we, the ordinary citizens, went about in blissful ignorance until one got embroiled one way or the other, as was inevitable. Fast forward to the Nigerian Civil War: partly because the easterners felt marginalised in their own country, they began to plot a secessionist underground movement, culminating in a full-blown war in 1967.

In January 1966, some senior Nigerian officers, mainly from the Igbo ethnic group, staged a coup and assassinated key politicians, including Ahmadu Bello, a revered leader in the North. This assassination led to months of massacres against the Igbos (including other southerners as they could not differentiate between them) living in the North. Tens of thousands were killed while about a million fled to what was then known as the Eastern region. These events sparked the decision to secede, spearheaded by Lt Colonel Ojukwu, the military governor of the Eastern region. In May 1967, Ojukwu declared the independence of the Federal Republic of Biafra. In July 1967, the government of Nigeria declared war on Biafra, which raged for two and a half years until January 1970, when Ojukwu fled the country, and Biafra surrendered. The leader of the federal government, General Yakubu Gowon, famously declared 'no victor, no vanquished' in the war. Adaobi Tricia Nwaubani has given an excellent analysis of the timeline of the war in her BBC article online.[14]

The day Julie was evacuated from her boarding school started like any other day in the dormitory. Students woke up to the morning bell and rushed into the shower rooms, then the chapel. They were coming out of the dining room when they were heralded into the assembly hall by the teachers and school matron and put into groups which they later found to be according to their destinations. They could see the long line of vehicles waiting outside, which was unusual. Students did not know what was happening because they had no radios or mobile phones then; contact with family was by letters in those days.

The headteacher then announced that a war had broken out, and they were all on their way home that instant. Some of the girls started to cry, especially the youngest ones like Julie, who was in the first year of secondary school. They were not allowed to return to the dormitory

---

[14] Adaobi Tricia Nwaubani, 'Remembering Nigeria's Biafra war that many prefer to forget' (15 January 2020), *BBC News*: https://www.bbc.co.uk/news/world-africa-51094093 (accessed: 4 September 2021).
.

to take any property. The priority was getting students home safely to their parents. They realised the enormity of the situation; the possibility of students being trapped in rebel territory and never being seen again by their parents. Reverend Sister Perpetua, an Irish nun, and the headteacher of Mary Mount College, Agbor, had gone to the motor park with other teachers to arrange for vehicles to come into the school to take the students back home to their different destinations in a convoy where possible. Julie was lucky to have come from the state's capital city, where most vehicles were headed in convoy.

The Nigerian War had broken out that day in response to the earlier announcement in May by Lt Colonel Odumegwu Ojukwu, declaring this part of the country to be part of a new country called Biafra. Biafra was declared to be a sovereign nation and seceded from Nigeria. The rebel soldiers were already in positions all over the Eastern parts of the country and the Mid-Western state. Sister Perpetua's action to get the children home to their parents safely on the day was highly commended. They were told later that another 24 hours' delay in making that decision would have been a disaster, as the roads became closed to free movement. They were urgently rushed into vehicles, panicking because the war had broken out in the region.

The journey was perilous and precarious through heavily armed Biafran army checkpoints. The soldiers dramatically ordered all of them out of the vehicles at various stops, checked the car's boot, or just peeped menacingly into the vehicles with their machine guns pointing in whatever direction they chose before letting them continue the journey. They had left all their property behind and arrived home with just their green check uniform on their backs. Julie was lucky to have travelled in the direction away from the war's epicentre, Eastern Nigeria. They heard later that some schoolchildren didn't make it safely home. Children in private cars with their fathers travelling deeper into rebel territory had their cars confiscated. The fathers were conscripted into the army, and some girls disappeared, never to be seen again.

Julie has never forgotten the sequence of events that unfolded from that point on, as seen through her young eyes. Julie didn't return to that school after the war ended. She remained in the Catholic boarding school, St Maria Goretti Girls' Grammar School in Benin City, where she and the other returnees remained during the war, having taken the places of the girls who had left in a hurry to travel into rebel territory (Biafra). All Indigenes of Igbo land were ordered back to their homeland; the exodus had started months earlier. All roads leading to the east of Nigeria were clogged with cars, buses, lorries, and cargo vehicles. Some were going back with much hope and optimism, beeping their horns continuously with thumbs up out of the car windows, while others were sad and sceptical and sorry to leave, judging by their countenance. Adults and children lined the main roads to watch the spectacle of this mass movement of people, which was of a biblical proportion.

The most painful part of this saga for families was being torn apart by war. There were lots of mixed marriages between Igbo people and other ethnic groups. Families had to decide who stayed and who went to the East. The question was, should they go alone or take the family with them? Some mixed marriages had adult children, further complicating things for the families. Some Ibo men left with some adult children, leaving their wives and younger children behind until things were more settled.

In some cases, those left behind never saw their loved ones again; they did not survive the war. Schools closed during the onset of the crisis while the federal government embarked on their military response to the occupation and secession. At some point, as the federal troops approached Benin City, some families fled the cities and towns for remote villages to avoid the onslaught. It was a time of confusion and chaos for many people.

On 6 July 1967, Julie was 11 years old when the war started as the Nigerian government had declared war on Biafra. The Mid-Western state with Benin City as its capital was now harnessed as part of Biafra. She found herself in an occupied territory, even though she was not from the Igbo tribe or their region. The Biafran army captured Benin and the other midwest cities on 9 August 1967. The Nigerian troops entered Benin on 20 September 1967. The Midwest Invasion lasted one month, one week and four days, and that was the end of the 'Republic of Benin', which Ojukwu had declared on 19 September 1967. The ambition of Biafra was to harness more regions than theirs to become occupied territories in addition to Biafra.

The Mid-Western state was therefore used as a buffer zone and became an occupied territory. The federal soldiers were approaching from the west towards the east to retake the Biafra territory but had to liberate the Mid-Western state first as it was sandwiched between them. The occupation of the Mid-Western region turned residents against the secessionist cause and was used by the Nigerian government as justification to escalate the war against Biafra.[15] On that day of the liberation of Benin by the federal troops, Julie witnessed the horrors of the Biafran War and what it did to people.

War is a gruesome business as can be seen in the aftermath of the fighting between the two armies. Many properties and buildings were destroyed, and many innocent civilians became casualties of the crossfire. The approaching federal army entered Benin City on 20 September 1967 to liberate the people from the Biafran army, the city having been occupied for one month and one week. Julie happened to be caught up in it while visiting her grandmother. There were bombs and shelling from opposite sides of the town, and homes and civilians were caught up in it. Everyone was trapped wherever they were, 'taking cover', as we called it, by lying flat on the floor and avoiding multi-storey buildings.

The federal soldiers pushed back the Biafran army and drove them out of town to liberate Benin City that day. As soon as people realised they were freed, there was mass hysteria as they streamed out of their houses into the streets, jubilant amid the destruction around them. Julie's grandma never knew that she sneaked out of the house with the other neighbourhood kids to join the street jubilations on the main street, and then suddenly, the

---

[15] Wikipedia, 'Nigerian Civil War':
https://en.wikipedia.org/wiki/Nigerian_Civil_War#Nigerian_offensive
(accessed on 23 February 2021).

sounds of war were brought starkly home in their presence.

People were rounding up their innocent civilian neighbours and bringing them to the soldiers shouting, 'See Ibo, see Ibo.' Julie witnessed the shooting of men and can never forget the image of a man in a white shirt lying on the ground, balanced on his left elbow while his right hand was waving frantically in the air, begging for his life. He was shot to loud cheering and applause from the onlookers. War shows us that mob brutality is universal and can lead people to commit the most dastardly and barbaric acts against fellow human beings.

Julie can still see the tanks as they rolled onto the main road called Mission Road. The soldiers jumped out, covered in artificial green leaves streaming down their helmets. They carried machine guns, shooting sporadically into the air to loud applause and cheering. They were being hailed as liberators from annexation to Biafra. The crowd surged forward to mob and embrace the soldiers, but Julie stayed back, petrified of the very dark huge men waving machine guns about and shooting sporadically into the air. It was speculated that the soldiers did not look like Nigerians but rather mercenaries recruited from neighbouring countries.

Julie pulled back and turned around to start running back home. At this point, her grandmother appeared from nowhere to pull her all the way home by the ear. She had mobilised an army of her own to look for Julie. What would she tell her daughter if anything happened to the grandchild under her watch? Curiosity took Julie back the following morning to the shooting scene of the previous day. The most traumatising and painful memory for her was finding that the man in the white shirt was still wriggling and alive. No one helped him because they were scared or did not know what to do. Julie could see the awe and gloom on people's faces as they stared blankly ahead with their hands crossed over their chests in shock, as the reality of the situation struck home. There was no jubilation there at that spectacle.

A new day had dawned, and the reality of what had happened the previous day had now hit home. The innocent civilian was left to die a slow and painful death. It still brings a tear to Julie's eye. It must also be said that many people risked their lives to hide their Ibo friends and neighbours, some for years, throughout the war. Some were caught during that early 'victory' euphoria and paid the ultimate price for trying to help their friends as they, too, were dragged out of the house and executed. No questions were asked. They only had to be Ibo or a friend of Ibo to be killed then. This carnage and senseless loss of life were supposed to be collateral damage necessary for freedom from oppression. Many heroic stories abound of people and churches who hid their Ibo friends and family throughout the war and moved them from one place to another at night.

Innocent civilian casualties were caught up in the crossfire, and many homes were destroyed by the shelling, which went on for hours. The Biafran side had foreign mercenaries, some of whom were Europeans who were later displayed on national television when caught. Julie remembers one of them saying in an interview that he did not care about the war. He was paid to fight. During the fight to liberate Benin, one of Julie's friends was hit inside her home on the first floor by a stray bullet and had her leg amputated at the age of 10.

The war raged on for another two and a half years, but it was now confined to Eastern Nigeria. The rest of the country watched it on blurry black-and-white TV or listened to the radio. One saw what the federal government wanted the country to see. Most of the time, it was a propaganda war of words in which they denied war crimes as reported by the foreign media. Most people huddled around radios to listen to BBC overseas news, the only way to get another perspective of what was happening in Biafra. Julie had grown up before she had the benefit of seeing the war through the lenses of outsiders. She watched documentaries on the Biafran War, which showed the devastation the war had caused in the region, especially the plight of the children who had died of hunger and starvation.

Many refugees were air-lifted out by charities to foreign countries at the time. There were shortages of food, basic amenities, and adequate medical supplies. When the war ended, friends returned from Biafra without their fathers, mothers and children who had died in the war. Some of the girls survived with the soldiers, and many returned with babies of dead soldiers. The community rallied to help them, as many of the young men who had been conscripted into the army had died. Those who returned were penniless because the federal government had changed the currency and made cash hoarded in rebel territory not legal tender and useless.

Julie's godmother, Theresa, came back a shadow of her previous bubbly and confident self. She returned from Biafra without her husband, son, father or mother, as they had all died in the war. She and her two daughters survived. They found their bungalow in a bad state but were lucky that unscrupulous land speculators had not demolished it and rebuilt it for themselves. They took back possession of the property from squatters, and the whole community rendered help to resettle them. Before the war, she had been a primary school teacher and the Girl Guides organiser at the convent primary school for girls where she taught.

Biafra lost the war and remained part of Nigeria, although murmurings of secession have been redoubled in recent years. Nigeria's problems have not improved with the politicians fanning the flames of division due to their religious bigotry, tribalism, lack of patriotism or simply corruption at the highest offices that has simmered down and become the plague of the citizenry. Nigeria has not come up with a leader to take the country forward. The country is going backwards. Infrastructure like light, water, schools, airways, the economy, and healthcare are collapsing. No leader has come up to inspire people, and hope, chaos, and desperation reign.

There was a time in Nigeria when there was no queuing at the post office, bus stops, etc.; civil servants went late to work or did not show up at all, and there was indiscipline at all levels coupled with moral decadence. Then came a military leader called General Idiagbon. He made the right threats, and suddenly, Nigerians were queuing in public places, not fighting, and civil servants were early to work for fear of being caught out. We proved that discipline could reign, but this state of affairs did not last; it all deteriorated after that regime, and the country lacked visionary leaders.

Belfast in the 1980s

Julie got married in August 1980 at the age of 25 to a young doctor, Isaac, who took her from Nigeria to Northern Ireland, only to find herself in another kind of war: the sectarian conflict between Catholics and Protestants in Northern Ireland. The 'Troubles' or the 'Northern Ireland Conflict' was dubbed a low-level war.[16] Isaac was a trainee doctor there at the time.

Her family, and Julie herself, were very worried about the prospect of living in Belfast. Back home in Nigeria, people did not understand the politics of the war. All they knew was that there was a war going on there, so long as random bombs were going off and people were being maimed and killed by them. So, Julie's parents were not happy that they were living in Belfast at that time. She was there when Bobby Sands (and nine other prisoners) died of a hunger strike in 1981 after being sentenced for firearms possession and protesting the removal of special category status. The city of Belfast was divided into a Loyalist and a Republican area, and the only common grounds were the hospitals and the city centre. Even then, people were often evacuated from shops after the police received anonymous calls of a parcel left behind some place or another.

One of the most unforgettable events of the war for Julie was when a Nigerian student (whose brother later became a close family friend) died on a train travelling from the South of Ireland to Belfast at Dunmurry, as a bomb went off prematurely, killing the carrier and others

---

[16] Wikipedia. *The Troubles.* (Accessed on 15 Mar 2021) at: https://en.wikipedia.org/wiki/The_Troubles

on the train on 17 January 1980. The Nigerian student was on a Master's degree course in Dublin. That brought it closer to home, and this news was widely broadcast internationally. Julie's social life was very restricted as her friends stayed home or held home parties. Visits to pubs were risky because it was always in her mind that a bomb could go off at any time. People lived in fear of being caught up in violence.

One day, Julie, her husband and her baby visited a family friend in County Armagh, about 40 miles from Belfast. On the way home, there was rioting, and it took several frantic turns on the streets for them to make it home. They could see the smoke billowing in the skies above the houses, the flickering fires from burning tyres and the riots ahead. Panicked motorists and pedestrians were making U-turns with their vehicles and turning into side streets while looking for a way to escape the area and the fire that threatened to envelop them. They finally made it to their apartment safely, but not before Julie's heart had flipped a thousand times out of fear that gripped them every time they turned a corner and saw the demonstrators or burning fires.

Julie was a postgraduate student at Queen's University in 1980, and for her dissertation, the university arranged for her to go to a school in the Catholic area. There was graffiti everywhere depicting the conflict, but Julie was not scared because she was a Catholic and felt comfortable going into the Catholic area. While at university, fellow students were very good to her as she had recently arrived from Africa and was on in-service training from the Ministry of Education in Nigeria.

Julie could not tell who was Protestant or Catholic, but her friends told her they could tell, due to the religious divide at the time! Her best friends in the class were two sisters who were teachers at a Catholic school in Ballymena. They all went to the pub together on Fridays after a busy week, had a pub dinner, a few drinks, and gambled on horses. It was a lovely group to have belonged to.

Ongoing wars

This generation hears of wars going on in different parts of the world from time to time. Take the wars that happened (or are still happening): the Biafran War in Nigeria; in Rwanda between the Tutsis and the Hutus; Pakistan and India; Iraq and Iran; civil wars in Afghanistan, Yemen, Syria, Libya and, more recently, Russia invaded Ukraine on 24 February 2022 and the war is still raging. In all these cases, people know the territory and who their enemies are, but a new kind of war has emerged that knows no boundaries and enemies are invisible. Nowadays, there are never-ending wars with invisible enemies like suicide bombers. The attack on the Twin Towers on 11 September 2001, dubbed 9/11, is one case. It was a series of four coordinated terrorist attacks by Al-Qaeda against the United States.

In the United Kingdom, on 7 July 2005 (7/7), four suicide bombers with rucksacks full of explosives killed 52 people and injured hundreds more. It was the worst single terrorist atrocity on British soil. On 22 May 2017, an Islamist extremist suicide bomber detonated a homemade bomb as people were leaving the

Manchester Arena after an Ariana Grande concert in which 23 people died, including children, and which left more than 800 people injured. This bombing was an act of terrorism in the name of religion. The same problem started in Nigeria with the insurgence of Boko Haram, a militant Islamist group fighting to create an Islamic state. The insurgence of Boko Haram in recent years as a 'religious' war negates everything that every religion stands for. They have allegedly been engaging in acts like kidnapping young girls from boarding schools, burning churches, and killing Christian religious leaders.

Even where there are no wars, there is a siege on a specific part of the population in the form of dastardly attacks that blight people's lives. For example, much-publicised police killings of Black people in America, such as the very public murder of George Floyd in Minneapolis on 25 May 2020 by the police for a minor misdemeanour that was escalated by the police. Many of these police shootings and killings were believed to be motivated by racial profiling, which disproportionately targets Black people.

Racist attacks make the Black person always feel in a state of war. Black people feel embattled and have no 'freedom' of movement for fear for their lives due to harassment and attack, especially in some parts of America where Blacks may 'stray' into the 'wrong' neighbourhood with dire consequences. Sadly, the violence today is just as bad as in history. People do not want to tolerate others they feel are different, and the politicians fan this flame of division to the point that we think that what divides us is more than the commonality. Julie fears for her children and grandchildren and prays that common humanity will prevail and the world will unite.

Julie finds herself worrying more than usual about the problems in the world. Maybe when one has children and grandchildren, one sees the world through different lenses and experiences, worrying about what the future holds for them. One hears of ethnic cleansing, genocide, wars, suicide bombers, mass shootings, etc. Unfortunately, in this age of digital technology, we are exposed to very graphic images of extreme violence, images that make one question man's inhumanity to man. The world seems to have learnt nothing from the past. It is almost a case of one step forward and two steps backward. For Julie, the challenge for everyone is how to protect, restore and promote our shared humanity.

Some people are clever, some not so clever, which applies to all races.

Patricia Iredia

The Journey Continues

Chapter 8

AIM HIGHER

Every minority group believes there seems to be a glass ceiling for all marginalised groups, whether men, women, or children. Julie is a Black African woman and so is in double jeopardy. 'The odds are stacked firmly against you,' says her white friend Martha, jokingly. Julie is an African but has an English name because she was a 'colonial' child, as she told her dentist when he asked her from where she got her name. He knew that all her children had African names as they were also his patients. In those days, when being baptised into the Catholic Church, one had to have a 'Christian' name compulsorily, which meant the names of saints in the Bible.

The Church has since capitulated on this doctrine to include all Christian names, irrespective of the language. African names can also be Christian, like Julie's middle name, 'Osariemen', which means 'God's gift' in the Edo language. God is 'Osa' or 'Osalobua' (God almighty). This dilemma is easy to understand when one understands that some African traditional religions worship the 'God of iron', and name children accordingly after these deities. For example, 'Igbinogun' translates literally as 'I cling to the God of iron.'

Julie was indoctrinated with the idea that the odds were stacked against her. This belief was her mindset when she arrived in her adopted country. She soon realised that people were the same everywhere, divided by religion, geographical regions, tribes, language, social class and colour. Most of the time, these differences, especially about a person's colour and ability, are mere stereotypes, not reality. Some people are clever, some not so clever, which applies to all races. 'Not so', according to those who want to malign others, sow division and hold on to a superiority complex.

Julie once took an online survey on social class for fun, and from her responses (some of which were not quite true as she answered 'no' to the question 'do you visit theatres and museums?' when she does in fact sometimes visit theatres, art galleries and museums), she discovered that she was considered low-class simply because of the activities she chooses to engage in, with no theatres, galleries, polo, golf, horse racing, cruising, etc. So, people are sharply divided on who and what they consider worthy of their attention and who deserves or does not deserve privileges that are fundamental human rights. Some hold beliefs of superiority and the privileges ingrained in that belief while demonising others as inferior, with the consequential assumptions about capabilities and possibilities. These assumptions seem to be in people's psyche and can come across in how they relate to others, and individuals can even end up with low expectations of the self with the consequent low achievement from that.

Julie was determined that her children would not grow up with this mindset of thinking that the odds were stacked against them, and they had their dad Isaac to look up to as well for inspiration. Her husband, Isaac, came to the UK as a young man to join his older brother, and they both accomplished all they set out to achieve academically. They had to ignore all the carrying on around them and focus on their lives and plans for achievement. They knew what they had come here for, and nothing was going to stop them. This determination guided his older brother to quickly complete his course and training as a quantity surveyor.

After graduation, his older brother went back home to Nigeria. He had a successful career as a quantity surveyor there, but Isaac stayed behind because of the length of training required for the course he had chosen to pursue, which was medicine. He, therefore, had to stay to complete his education and specialist training and thereafter decided to stay and work in the UK.

He had many stories to tell about his experiences as someone who came into this country as an adult. Having grown up in Nigeria, he was confident in himself and his abilities. He had a grade one in his Ordinary-level (O-level) and excellent Advanced-level examinations (A-level, British examinations), and he was a Head Boy at his secondary school, which achievements speak volumes for his abilities and character. He had not grown up in a system that subjugated him to believe that he was a second-class citizen, discriminated against, or made to feel that he could not achieve his goals. He had pride in himself and his royal heritage through his mother, a princess. She was called 'Uvbi', which means 'princess' in the Edo language. Like most of his generation, he was resolute in pursuing his goals and did not perceive any obstacle could rob him of his ambitions. So, he went about his pursuits with positivity that enabled him to ignore most negative experiences, especially racist ones. There were times when he knew that the outcome of his effort as judged by others, when compared to that of his contemporaries, was unfairly below par, but he took it all in his stride and just forged ahead to the next task, the final goal being 'to succeed and hold that certificate in my hands', to use his own words.

When his generation came here as British Commonwealth citizens, they did not need a visa, and he and his counterparts did whatever they had to do to survive. At one point, Isaac lived in a dump of a room where heating was non-existent, as that was what he could afford. The landlord told them he put on heating once yearly 'on shower day'. He was doing three jobs and saving up for his education, especially as it would be more difficult to work during the years of clinical study. The tenants were all young men from a hot country who showered twice or more daily. It made more sense to be doing three jobs to keep busy, have warmth and even free hot food if one happened to be working in a restaurant. He worked in a toy factory overnight and on Oxford Street, London, in the early hours at a Savile Row shop as a cleaner for two hours before opening time and then went to university from there. He recounted how hot tears were the only warmth he felt one day, trudging through the deep snow back from the factory where he had worked overnight. All he could see through the tears were the streetlights glistening against the white canvas that foggy morning.

There was also the story of the humane manager who caught him studying his medical textbook during his break and could not believe that anyone working there had any ambitions to further their education beyond working in the factory for life. That was when Isaac told him he was a medical student at King's College, University of London, and had classes in the morning. He usually showered and changed in the factory. He needed money to pay his school fees, buy his books and maintain himself. From that day onwards, that Jewish manager made his life 'easier' by letting him sneak off to sleep for an hour and letting him off an hour early sometimes and so on. Some people he came across along the way helped him to succeed. Isaac never forgot such kindness from another human being. He always went back to look for the manager long after he had graduated and left the area.

The doctor who helped him enter the system was an Englishman Isaac went to for advice when he first arrived in the UK. It took him more than 20 visits before he could get past a nasty and racist secretary to see the consultant doctor who was the adviser of international students of his institution. The boss came out of the office one day, saw him again in the waiting room, and asked him to come in. That meeting changed his life. It was that man who advised Isaac about what selection exams to take to get into the system, and he just took him under his wing from there on, even making phone calls on his behalf to relevant agencies and colleges. He was amazed at Isaac's determination to see him and ask for help after going to the library to search through London's medical schools' staff job descriptions; Isaac was looking for someone who mentored international students. Isaac never stopped talking about the man who gave him a break. Twenty years after their encounter, Isaac looked him up in their doctors' journal and sent him a box of wine through *The Times*' wine list with a thank-you card.

That generation succeeded because they did not see themselves as 'victims' or 'scroungers', as they were described by others, but more like adventurers. They came here to work and educate themselves, not to collect benefits, and most succeeded in their quest. Isaac's generation was strong because of their strong foundations. It was not easy to convince someone who did not grow up with an inferiority complex to now feel inferior. They found that suggestion ludicrous because they were proud and intelligent young men with 'drive' and purpose in life. That was why they could absorb the system's shock better when they came here. It was a case of 'I know who I am.'

Isaac re-told the story of one of his professors who asked him what in his background made him so confident in himself. Maybe, he was not as timid as expected for a newbie from Africa. Isaac replied that he grew up with strong family support, was good at school, and was a Head Boy. He never hesitated when faced with challenges but always believed he could do something or at least tried his best. He had his share of discrimination regarding job availability and the selection processes, but all said and done, he had many more positive experiences to speak of. Most people were always ready to help him succeed, but there were others who liked to put obstacles in the way to make things look insurmountable.

Isaac told his children these stories to inspire and motivate them, even though, unfortunately, their circumstances were different. These children were born here in the UK. They have never experienced the 'freedom' of being themselves and not being judged from the cradle for the colour of their skin. They were lucky to have lived in Nigeria for a while. The system gradually erodes their sense of self-worth, and it is an uphill battle in the homes telling these children, 'You are loved! You are important! You are equal to anyone in God's eyes.' That's not the message ethnic minority children are getting from their environment, not even from pews in some churches, the school playground, the classroom, on the streets, in the news or on the bus where they often have two seats to themselves, even when the bus is full. Top that list with all the negative images of Black people in the media whose eyes are covered in flies or being killed, and one will not wonder that Black kids struggle to believe they are equal human beings to white people. These children were born with the extra burden of always having to justify their relevance, their behaviour, abilities and even their very existence compared to their white counterparts who have no such burden.

Julie's children knew they had to succeed, no matter what the obstacles were on the way. The children had heard enough from their father that, if you are strong, 'No one can take your brain away from you. You must decide to block out all else and use it.'

Julie was a very supportive mother who also trumpeted the value of a good education, especially as she could boast of some certificates too. So, fortunately, they were brought up believing there were no obstacles in the way, as far as their academic achievement was concerned. Their parents showed them that education was the quickest way out of poverty. It was faster and surer than trying to be a football star or an artist. As Julie's late husband Isaac used to say, 'This is the route I know. I do not know about hustling, music or football or trying to be Picasso. These are possible, but this is the route I know.'

It had been drummed into their heads to make no excuses. In some African cultures, when a child fails in exams, there's always the convenience of blaming a stepmother or a significant other by accusing them of being witches who do not want them to succeed. In the UK, Black children can easily blame racism or say, 'The teacher does not like me.' This statement can also be said in Africa, but it is the frequency and consequences of it on different children that change.

Racism is an important factor in children's achievement because the children can see the double standards in how some teachers and the wider community treat them in a way that erodes their confidence and impedes their performance and progress. When a Black child is innovative in class, the teacher may put him or her down as being 'too' forward, getting ahead of themselves. The children always came home confused, claiming, '... but the teacher praised John ... and we had the same ...'. If they dare to exhibit confidence in their nature/nurture by how they speak or refuse to do an assignment in a particular way (like any 7-year-old might), they are quickly labelled as aggressive, uncooperative, etc.

The discrimination just never ends, and this leaves the children very confused. It is left to the parents at home to restore balance by reassuring the child that the teacher meant well and such pep talk because one does not want to raise a child who is anti-teacher or anti-establishment. It often breaks the adult's heart to see the confusion in the child. After all, they are just 7-year-olds who do not know about such concepts as racism or discrimination, but they start to experience it very early in life and describe it. How do you explain to a 7-year-old why his coat was found in the trash again in the cloakroom? The headteacher had to tell the child to leave his coat behind his chair and not with others on the coat hanger. This incident happened to Julie's child.

Julie recalls that, in her home while raising her kids, it was a deliberate policy always to be optimistic about everything, and it paid off. They understood that one cannot control the behaviour of others but can control one's own, which was also an important lesson to teach.

In the school system, it has been known that Black children are often asked, 'Did you do this assignment by yourself?' Teachers display disbelief that a Black child can produce a high-level project. Julie's child was asked that very question after she had worked so hard to produce an outstanding project at her secondary school. She is 40 years old now and still bitter about that experience. She was marked down because of the teacher's assumption that she could not have done it by herself. She knows she was marked down because the second teacher, who also supervised the project but did not mark it, told Julie that that was an A standard of work. That incident made the child very sad and discouraged, especially when it was obvious that other students were marked up and not down, even when they failed to complete the assignment with bogus excuses, which they boasted about to their friends.

However, her kids were taught to be consistent and resilient, and to prove themselves, never accepting a defeatist attitude.

'When you get a low mark, it is because you haven't worked hard enough,' says Julie.

Children in her house were not allowed to use the expression, 'The teacher gave me 40%.' No, you got 40%.

Julie quickly realised that, if you do not establish this mindset early on in life, that child will develop excuses for failure. It is a herculean task to build children's confidence in an environment that may sometimes be difficult or negative, but this is a task that must be done. Having confidence can come from having self-worth and not having an inferiority complex because of all the negative messages from the environment. So that another way to help her children excel in school was to bring them up to have a sense of worth. Julie would not call it high, medium, or low self-esteem, just self-worth. High or medium self-esteem is necessary for confidence and emotional well-being, but hard work should not be sacrificed on the ego of high self-esteem. Traditional study habits and perspiration will deliver exam success and, thereby, high self-esteem.

When it comes to self-esteem, many Black children growing up in a white-dominated environment have very high hurdles to jump over, judging by the number of negative stereotypes of Black people and negative images of people that look like them. Julie remembers how her children used to cringe at disgusting images of Black children covered in flies in the name of charity. It was for charity, but how does it help the cause if prospective donors are so disgusted that they do not even think it is worth watching or the kids are worth helping? Researchers and psychologists have shown a positive self-image in life to be positively associated with well-being and academic success. It is not in the scope of this essay to go into details of academic research.

The children themselves must want to achieve success by having self-determination to succeed and must want to engage in intellectual pursuits because of an intrinsic interest in learning. The children must enjoy learning new things and be prepared to put in the effort.

The tough tasks before parents are: how do you convince a child who is desperate to belong that wearing the latest Adidas or Nike shoe will not define who they are to be accepted by their peers? How do you keep them on the straight and narrow path? Confidence in who we are comes from within, and one can earn respect for one's accomplishments rather than by breaking one's neck to belong with the Joneses or to join gangs. Kids need friends but not those based on wearing the latest outfit, especially when the child cannot afford them.

'There are good children out there who have similar goals to yourself and who will accept you for who you are,' Julie used to say. 'I promise you when you've achieved your goals, you shall earn enough money to buy as many pairs of shoes as you want and whatever type or brand.'

At this juncture, the children could be told the success stories of kids who never started off being 'rich' or privileged or famous but achieved great things. Nowadays, Barack Obama, Michelle Obama and Oprah Winfrey are great role models for Black children, mainly because of their humble beginnings. Many ordinary Black folks around us are teachers, nurses, doctors, and shop owners who have succeeded at their chosen vocations and are positive role models for children, especially Black children.

Motivating children to excel takes a lot of determination and some good luck or divine intervention (for religious believers) in the values upheld by the children and everything coming together to make it happen. These values were not easy to teach or master, but Julie likes to think she succeeded because her kids were known for never accepting a 'B' as good enough, as the teachers told her. They always asked their teachers, 'What more can I do to get an A?' They were very accommodating and supportive. One of her daughters once reported that a teacher once told her, 'I don't want your father to come and kill me,' when giving her more work to do. It was hilarious, but it shows that teachers know parents who are interested in their children's academic performance in school and encourage them to work hard.

They soon realised that no one could stop them from achieving any height they were capable of, even if they tried. They just had to be resilient and work hard. It also helped that, being the only Black children in the school, they experienced positive discrimination most of the time.

Making friends also helped them to fit in. There were many hilarious moments growing up, like when her 5-year-old daughter was playing in the back garden of their new house, and the 5-year-old from the house at the back came to the fence. They faced each other across the fence and examined each other with some curiosity. Then the little white girl asked, 'Why are you black?'

Julie's daughter shrugged her shoulders and replied, 'I don't know. Why are you white?'

The little girl shrugged and replied with her shoulders raised and hands outstretched. 'I don't know.'

They both started giggling.

Another of Julie's daughter's friends commented, 'They've lied to me all my life. We are just the same!'

Help your children make friends across the races, which will help eradicate ignorance and prejudices.

Julie has taught her children to face the world with positivity. They have made some good friends and have done very well with their studies and careers, which is proof that with the right motivation, self-worth, belief in self, and hard work, one can succeed at school and shatter the glass ceiling while aiming for the sky. President Obama succeeded, despite the racism, discrimination and underestimation he experienced. Even his agent perceived his name as a disadvantage, but Obama refused to change it. One must stay positive and have the self-belief to succeed.

AN IMMIGRANT CHILD

Who am I?

An African child.

Red blood runs in my vein.

Black skin defines me.

Kinky hair in the bargain.

I can still hear Africa

Drumming in my ears.

I can hear Grandma's laughter,

the sound of pounding yam,

and the chatter of bustling children.

I can smell the dusty rain.

I can smell roasted plantains

and hot chilli beans.

I can smell roasted corn and peanuts.

Stranger to my ancestral home;

Stranger in my adopted country.

Sad and hungry eyes stare at me;

Smiley faces, angry faces, glare at me.

Who am I?

Funny questions, curious questions,

Honest questions, rude questions,

Thrown at me.

Do you eat tomatoes?

Do you eat chilli?

Is your blood red?

Where do you come from?

Why did you come here?

What are you doing here?

The struggle to just live goes on.

The struggle to belong.

The struggle to understand.

The struggle to be understood.

The struggle to have faith in humanity.

The struggle to have faith in God.

Who am I?

A child created by God.

A child of the universe.

An Immigrant Child.

Patricia Iredia

The home must be a loving, stable, nurturing home so that children can better face the realities in the world.

Patricia Iredia

Chapter 9

HELPING BLACK CHILDREN SUCCEED IN SCHOOL

Discussing how to help Black students succeed in school brings us to a unique social variable, racism. Racism against Black people in the Western world can potentially impact students' motivation, self-esteem and self-belief or the way they process their successes or failures, and thereby their ability to thrive in school and their environment. This impact of racism on the self-esteem of students is not a factor in Nigeria, as all the children are of the same race. All the other variables affecting educational success, such as parental nurture, poverty, school policies, infrastructure, bullying, teachers and guidance counsellors, are the same everywhere one goes.

Many reports and research have shown the negative impact of racism and discrimination on Black kids' academic success and general well-being. In the UK, for example, racism is an identifiable debilitating issue that faces Black and other ethnic minority children every day, starting from a very young age. Sally Weale reports research by YMCA, which found that most Black children report experiencing racism at school.[17] Asked about racism in education, more than 9 out of 10 (95%) said they had witnessed racist language at school, and almost half (49%) said they believed racism was the most significant barrier to academic attainment.

There was an incident that occurred when one of her children carried out a project in which she had to take photographs in the wild. There were no mobile phones then, so she had to purchase a camera and then went to the park to take her photos. She printed the photos, wrote her essay, and even bound the project with a transparent plastic folder. For some reason, she had two teachers looking at the same project. The one who marked it asked her, 'Did you do this project yourself, or did your father do it for you?' She marked it a B, at which the other supervisor was mortified. She told the young girl that would have been a definite grade A effort if she had marked the paper. The irony was that her white

[17] S. Weale, 'RACE: Most Black British children report experiencing racism at school' (29 October 2020), *The Guardian*: https://www.theguardian.com/world/2020/oct/29/most-black-british-children-report-experiencing-racism-at-school (accessed : 20 October 2021).

friend could not be bothered to finish the assignment and submitted a half-completed assignment with a sob story that she was sick and was given an A. That teacher could not bring herself to believe that a Black student could produce a high-quality assignment, despite her parents' high academic qualifications and ethos.

This story may not reflect what every teacher will do to a Black child, but it certainly depicts the extra challenges that Black children must face to jump the hurdles. A range of institutional practices undermines Black students' performance at school, such as punishment and exclusion from school and bullying by teachers and peers.

There are not enough teachers from diverse backgrounds, and even the few that exist suffer untold hardships and discrimination in the system, as narrated by Oppoi,[18] a Black teacher who was forced into early retirement because of the racism she faced from peers and the authorities. It is worse for students who have no recourse to justice should they want to complain.

The discrimination in the wider society is glaring and exemplified in police practices and how Black children are treated across the justice system. This social injustice is an extensive topic beyond the scope of this essay. One thing is certain, though, that things have got to change to improve the lives of ethnic minority children growing up in this society where institutional racism and discrimination prevent some from achieving academic success and reaching their full potential. They

---

[18] M. Osei-Oppong, *For the Love Of Teaching in Education: The Anti-Racist Battlefield in Education*. Peaches Publications, 2020.

sometimes work twice as hard as their white counterparts and are still not judged good enough by some teachers.

There is the adage that charity begins at home. The home has a significant role to play in how a child develops physically, vocationally, emotionally, and psychologically. Parents of Black children must raise their children to be positive and go-getters, to be resilient and not develop a victim mentality, as that would be counterproductive. The home must be a loving, stable, nurturing home so that children can better face the realities in the world. If your child comes home and says, 'The teacher gave me 40%', the immediate response should be, 'No, the teacher did not give you 40%; you got 40%!' High self-esteem does not guarantee good grades, but the converse is true – good grades lead to high self-esteem. Parents must encourage traditional hard work, which will lead to academic success.

Teachers also have a role to play in students' academic success in their classrooms. Respect for the individual, good teaching and encouragement are the bedrock of student success. The right curriculum by policymakers and eradicating disproportionate exclusions, racism and discrimination from the school and society will help ensure that all students feel valued and included.

SAY NO TO BULLIES

Bullies are cowards, so do not be scared.

Bullies are wicked; oh, do not be fazed.

Bullies are liars. Stay true to yourself.

Bullies are selfish, but you must stay kind.

Bullies put you down, but keep your head up.

Bullies do not own you; you own yourself.

Put Bullies to shame by being resilient.

Put the Bullies to shame by being strong.

Put the Bullies to shame by keeping cool.

Put the Bullies to shame with confidence.

Put the Bullies to shame; be courageous.

Put the Bullies to shame; be successful.

Know who you are. Be proud of who you are.

Know who you are. Be proud of what you are.

Know who you are. Be happy with your best.

Know who you are, a shining light from God.

Know who you are, unique and different.

Know who you are. Say NO to the Bully.

Patricia Iredia

Go for it. Go for whatever you want. Don't let anybody or anything stop you.

Patricia Iredia

Chapter 10

COVID-19

Preamble

If it was possible to know when one would die, we could plan for it. Unfortunately, it has not been possible for scientists or spiritualists or soothsayers, with all their knowledge, to have an answer to this question of humankind's mortality. Referring to death, the Bible states in Ecclesiastes 9:12 (NIV):

> Moreover, no one knows when their hour will come:
>
> As fish are caught in a cruel net,
> or birds are taken in a snare,

so people are trapped by evil times
that fall unexpectedly upon them.

Since the issue of Covid-19 started, everyone has been consumed with the fear of getting infected and possibly dying. We read in the news about a surge in people scrambling to write their wills and prepare for the unknown. All we heard on the news was coronavirus-related. Who has died, who is infected, and who has recovered? The grim prognosis we had at the beginning was of worse to come, with the different waves of the infection ahead of us. Some did not die but have become incapacitated for life with the complications of the virus.

This virus is no respecter of persons. It has infected heads of state, prime ministers, kings, princes, influencers, men, women, and children, sometimes with devastating effects. The news was dominated by information about coronavirus; at some point, it was like hourly updates from the government, announcements of new rules, U-turns, and so on. It was all very complicated and confusing at the beginning. For instance, it was sometimes very confusing to interpret the 'stay at home to work' rule. Despite the serious message of the announcement, this was also a time when people had some funny TikTok memes circulating on social media, and they went viral.

This coronavirus took the world by surprise; no one saw it coming, and it is still debated when and how it started. There has been speculation that it started in Wuhan in China, around the end of 2019, but this is disputed by China. It was not until January 2020 that governments worldwide became aware that a rogue virus was spreading. The first lockdown in the UK started on 16 March 2020. It was shocking when everything shut down, and no human contact outside the immediate family was possible. The devasting effect of these measures on people and businesses is still reverberating today. Thousands of people became scared of losing their jobs, and many did, and many small businesses and even big ones could not withstand the pressure of closure and soon terminated business. People were suffering from anxiety and depression more than usual.

Schools were closed, and eventually, parents were saddled with teaching their children at home and doing their full-time jobs. Parents working from home or going out to work, like frontline workers, became teachers as well. A new culture was born, working from home for those who could. There was a glossary of words associated with the new 'normal' life of Covid-19: social distancing, quarantine, lockdown, endemic, pandemic, antibodies, herd immunity, test and trace, self-isolation, and bubbles. The government introduced new slogans at different stages of the pandemic. Below are examples of some of the jargon adopted by the prime minister:

Stay Home. Protect the NHS. Save Lives.

Stay Alert! Control the Virus. Save Lives!

Wash hands. Cover face. Make space.

Eat out to help out.

Rule of Six.

I have been talking about Covid-19 as if everyone reading this right now, or perhaps 30 years from now, knows what it is. Someone in the generation to come who did not live through this may never know what it is, not even as much as my 3-year-old grandson knows now. His dad told him to get ready to go to the park for a walk, and he started screaming that he did not want to go there 'because there's a lockdown there. Covid will catch you!'

The not knowing is not surprising. It is the same as when some in this generation asks the questions: 'What is Spanish flu? What is pandemic influenza H1N1 virus?'

Many people did not know that there had been a pandemic a century ago, in 1918. That discourse was often left to the history books and history documentaries or the occasional mention in medical discussions on news bulletins. When the photographs surfaced, it was surreal to see people wearing face masks in black-and-white pictures from a long time ago.

One of the most defining issues of quarantine and lockdown was the worsening mental health crisis because of isolation, fear of contracting the disease or the thought of losing a loved one, the state of the economy, fear of losing one's job, and actual job losses. The situation was very stressful for many people, especially those living alone, causing anxiety, lethargy, and depression.

Human beings are social animals; when cut off from family, friends and grandchildren and the whole world shuts down around them, they struggle to cope. Besides mental health implications, it also impacts one's physical health. Talking to people, you find that migraine, piles, backache, and obesity increased. Working from home also meant that people were seated on their chairs for longer than they would previously have been. Pottering around the house while on a break does not replace the adrenalin of jumping out of bed in the morning, getting ready to go to work, jumping on buses and trains or driving. People tried to do the right thing by walking where possible, but there is no doubt that the lockdown meant reduced mobility for everyone, which affected our mental and physical well-being.

During the lockdown, Julie was lucky not to be alone. Her daughter, son-in-law and their baby were supposed to be there for ten days to allow workers to renovate their house. The kitchen was ripped out. That was when the lockdown started, and they were stranded in Julie's house. Meanwhile, Julie came back from Africa two days before the lockdown. Her son was also home from the university, where he was a mature medical student. During the lockdown, he worked as a pharmacist, and every one of her children was a frontline worker.

While it was good to have company, it was also terrifying for Julie and her pregnant daughter. Her daughter's husband was a hospital doctor and was exposed to Covid-19 daily at work. This exposure risk started when no medicines or reliable treatments were available to combat the disease. The cleaning routine that was set up in the house was rigorous. No shoes from the hospital or clothes were allowed in the house. The frontline staff in Julie's home had to change in the car, bag all their clothes, and take them straight to the washing machine daily. The shoes were left in the car. Everyone in the house was socially distanced from those coming in until they came out of the shower. All the effort must have paid dividends because nobody in the house caught it then, and they must have been lucky too.

It was a very stressful time for families, especially those with caring jobs. Julie suffered a lot from lack of sleep, headaches and night sweats, all symptoms of fear of the unknown, especially when the first wave of deaths were of BAME people. It was a miracle that everyone survived Covid-19, despite working in hospitals.

There were some good times when rules eased a bit, and Julie could drive to the next village to see her grandchildren from the car! They came out and stood at their door for social distance visits, and to avoid shouting, they spoke on the phone. It was something to laugh about at the time.

Covid-19: Julie's Nigerian experience

Julie travelled to Nigeria at the end of February 2020. The journey had been planned for months because it was for her niece's wedding in Benin City, Nigeria, which took place on the first Saturday of March 2020. The couple came in from America for the wedding, along with Julie's siblings, nieces, nephews, grandchildren, and friends who live all over America. Julie managed to be present for two family events because her brother-in-law died, and his funeral fell within the period of her stay. He had been the de-facto father to Julie's children since 2004, when her husband passed away. He played that role at four weddings for her children. Julie would have had to return to Nigeria twice, so it worked out well.

She booked a KLM return ticket from Glasgow to Lagos months in advance. At about the time of departure in late February, there were murmurings and rumours of a pandemic. The seriousness of the situation had not been recognised enough to lead to draconian measures. It was certainly not on the news bulletins or taken seriously in Nigeria. The bride was fortunate because no one knew what Covid-19 was at the time, or it would have been a different story. Tickets had been bought at least six months in advance, and everyone was hoping to meet again for a huge family reunion.

In recent years, weddings have allowed Julie and her relatives to meet as a family to see each other. As modern life dictates, Julie and her siblings now live on three different continents and are scattered in different countries within the continents. They vowed to support each other at every opportunity. Julie has been the greatest recipient of this arrangement because her siblings, nieces and nephews were there for her through 'five weddings and a funeral'. Most of those travelling from abroad arrived a week before the wedding date at the beginning of March. In the week before the wedding day and after arrival, people began to fall ill with fever, chills, extreme tiredness, headache, cough, lethargy, and fainting. Typically, in Nigeria, all fevers are 'associated' with malaria, which they suspected. Some suggested that it was the 'flu', but whatever it was, they attacked it vigorously with malaria medicines and vitamin C, and everyone eventually recovered fully. They had done a lot of weddings in the Easter holidays before but never had they had so many people fall ill at the same time. Julie had fever, chills, headache, extreme tiredness, and a cough. She and her cousin were living in the same house, and they could not get up for three days.

Another cousin came to Julie to collect a cheque to help withdraw money from the bank, but Julie could not even get up to write the cheque. She promised to come back the next day, only for Julie to get a phone call from her cousin's daughter to say, 'My mum is very sick. I don't know what is wrong with her. She cannot even get up.' That cousin and another cousin remained sick for weeks, long after the wedding party had left. They said the doctors asked them if they had been around people from abroad. So, the doctors were already clued-up as to what was developing in the news in the medical world.

Julie coughed through the airport and for about two weeks after she returned. When she spoke to her daughter from the airport in Lagos, her daughter was alarmed that Julie was coughing, but Julie put it down to her allergies. Her daughter was not convinced and told Julie that coughing was one of the symptoms of Covid-19, so she became very self-conscious on her journey back, wandering about at the airport looking for quiet corners to cough in, after holding it in for as long as she could. Julie's daughter told her to check the duty-free shop for face masks, but there were none. Then she noticed a middle-aged gentleman with a big portfolio, wearing a mask. She approached him to beg for a mask, and he opened his portfolio and gave one to her, for which she was grateful. Once again, her daughter asked if he had worn gloves before giving them to her, at which point Julie snapped at her to stop stressing her out. Now that she had got a mask, her daughter was scared that the giver might have contaminated it. At this point, Julie began to sense how bad things were in the UK. Her daughter rushed her back because it was already evident that a lockdown was imminent in the next few days.

That mask was Julie's saving grace on her journey back because other passengers did not find it funny that anyone was coughing at the airport or on the plane, especially at the stop-over at Heathrow Airport and on the London-Glasgow flight. All heads turned, and one got very angry stares anytime one coughed. Mine was a 'scratchy throat' kind of cough, but there were other passengers with loud and continuous coughs, and people reacted as if every cough was sinister. Julie's cough lingered for about two weeks after she got back, then stopped, and she has not coughed once since. She will never know whether her illness was coronavirus, but her niece in Lagos, who also fell ill, later tested positive for antibodies some months ago.

There was no sign in Nigeria that anything was amiss in the world. Everyone was going about their regular business, which was surprising for a country that had recently gone through Ebola and acted swiftly and successfully to the acclaim of the world community. As borders closed abroad, flight cancellations started to hit the wedding party, the first group being the Americans with European tickets. They were scrambling to buy a one-way return ticket from American airlines flying direct to America at crazy prices. It was all within a 48-hour travel period. They had jobs and families to return to in the US and had only planned to be away for 8 to 12 days.

At this point, Julie thought she would never suffer that fate as she lived in Europe. Barely 24 hours later, she received an email from KLM changing her travel details to one day earlier than her original departure date. A few hours later, she was still processing this information and thinking of how she would change her travel plans from Benin to Lagos when another email arrived cancelling the Amsterdam to Glasgow flight indefinitely. So, what would she do if she got stranded in Amsterdam then?

Once again, her daughter took charge of the situation. She decided there and then that she would get Julie a British Airways ticket to get her into the UK directly, and that was what she did. Needless to say, the one-way ticket was costly as the journey was less than 48 hours away. Julie remembers foolishly asking that she extend her time by one or two days since she was buying a new ticket which her daughter vehemently refused to do. She said, '… you don't understand; get out now. Tomorrow was your travel date; just leave on that date. Drop everything and leave.' Everyone realised that the rumours had become a reality and something serious was happening abroad. The first lockdown in the UK came into effect two days after Julie got back to Glasgow.

Her brother-in-law, who was travelling back to the US, was sitting with his sister on the plane when she suddenly became sick with vomiting and diarrhoea. He had to assist with the cleaning up. On getting to the United States, he too developed persistent diarrhoea and lethargy for about ten days before deciding to go and queue up for a Covid-19 test at the testing centre and subsequently tested positive for coronavirus. Luckily, he was already on the mend and went on to recover fully. He had taken malaria medication and vitamins when he felt unwell in Nigeria and the US. The family promptly prepared him some concoction that had been trending in the news, made up of garlic, ginger and lemon. He was fortunate to have recovered fully from the ordeal, and her sister and the entire family could breathe a sigh of relief.

Covid-19 has brought out the inter-connectedness between all of us. People everywhere were forced to rise and become one another's keepers. Governments, local councils, big and small businesses, churches, charities, and individuals rose to the challenge to help feed the vulnerable during the lockdown. The lockdown brought many challenges that were not there before. With the closure of hospitality, shops, cafes and restaurants, many casual workers became destitute. In Nigeria, many of the employees in this sector were daily paid workers; they may not have been rich, but they never had to beg before because they were prepared to string three jobs together to make ends meet. They may not have been the caterer, but they were the employees of the caterer, working as the cook, cleaner, waiter, salesperson and driver/delivery man. Thousands of people lost their means of livelihood without recourse to any other source of income to fend for their families.

It was a privilege to belong to a family group that put money together in a pot and distributed food parcels to extended family and friends in need. The hurriedly put-together 'charity' money pot is still in operation as participating members are encouraged to keep putting funds into it. The challenges are still there, and even though the country claims not to have recorded many Covid-19 patients, there has been an unusual spate of deaths recorded in recent times, due directly or indirectly to Covid-19. People have no money for food, basic medical supplies, or medicines, as many have lost their sources of income.

There is no welfare state; however, the government received a lot of corporate sponsorship to feed the masses, but the distribution logistics were chaotic and did not reach those who needed it. Some of the Covid-19 relief items marked as such, like baby milk, ended up in the open market. That was blatant corruption on display once again. There were cases of wealthy individuals filling up the equivalent of two football stadiums in every local government area all over the state with groceries and essential supplies, distributed door to door to households in poorer areas. They opened hot food kitchens feeding thousands daily during the lockdown. These individuals were an inspiration and a lesson to all to have compassion and to look after one another.

Here in the UK, a lot was going on also by charities, churches, local councils and government-funded schemes to help communities at the grassroots level. Charities were delivering hot food to people isolated in their homes. Food parcels were also being delivered to various groups; even tablet computers were provided by councils and distributed to people. Those who were elderly, single parents or asylum seekers got help buying phones or tablets to enable them to engage with others on Zoom. These heart-warming stories helped to distract one from all the alarming developments that were going on around us.

BAME workers

At the start of the pandemic, the first casualties were disproportionately Black, Asian, and Minority Ethnic (BAME) groups. The initial reaction from the government and scientists was that BAME people were more prone to die from the disease when infected. This news sent a wave of panic and fear through the concerned community. All Julie's children work on the front line, so this news greatly affected her, causing restless nights and heightened anxiety. Luckily, the narrative of BAME people being more prone to die from the disease was quickly debunked upon more knowledge and social analysis.

'Our statistical modelling shows that a large proportion of the difference in the risk of Covid-19 mortality between ethnic groups can be explained by demographic, geographical and socio-economic factors such as where you live or the occupation you are in,' said Ben Humberstone, the deputy director of the health and life events division at the Office for National Statistics (ONS).[19]

---

[19] Office for National Statistics, 'Updating ethnic contracts involving the coronavirus (COVID-19),England and Wales: deaths occurring 2 March to 28 July 2020' (16 October 2020):
https://www.ons.gov.uk/peoplepopulationandcommunity/birthsdeathsandmarriages/deaths/articles/updatingethniccontrastsindeathsinvolvingthecoronavirusCOVID19englandandwales/deathsoccurring2marchto28july2020 (accessed: 21 August 2021).

This new information gave great relief to the BAME community, who could then concentrate on keeping themselves safe with the knowledge that they are not more prone, just more exposed for the various reasons explained by the ONS.

Clap for carers

Despite the ills associated with Covid-19, some good was born out of some events. The National Health Service (NHS) staff and other keyworkers were very much appreciated and applauded for their dealing and bravery in working to save lives, unlike the fate of some nurses in Mexico who faced violent attacks and were being called names. It was uplifting and encouraging to all the NHS workers that millions of people came out to clap for them every Thursday. This tradition was started by Annemarie Plas, a Dutch national living in South London. The weekly clap was stopped after ten weeks on 28 May because the founder did not want it to become politicised.

Captain Tom

Captain Tom was another reason to smile during the pandemic. He brought the whole country together as we all watched him with admiration as he walked to raise money for NHS Charities Together. Captain Tom quickly became a social media phenomenon. He captured the hearts of everyone both at home and abroad and consequently achieved monumental success with his solo fundraising effort. Captain Tom launched a fundraiser for the NHS in April that involved walking 100 laps of his garden to mark his milestone 100 years birthday. He had initially set out to raise £1,000 for NHS charities but eventually raised £33 million. He received over 147,000 birthday cards from all over the world for his 100 years birthday. Captain Tom became a source of joy, hope and inspiration in the dark days of coronavirus. For his efforts, he was honoured by the Queen with a knighthood.

Jerusalema

Master KG and vocal artist Nomcebo Zikode from South Africa took the world by storm with their song, 'Jerusalema', during the isolation caused by Covid-19. It was amazing that a song from South Africa resonated with everyone worldwide, maybe because of its inherent religious theme. Jerusalema challenge and dance routines have become a viral dance phenomenon drawing on global audiences. Internationally, politicians, sports stars, priests, nuns and monks, shop attendants, and infinite global citizens have posted videos of themselves participating in group dancing, accepting the Jerusalema dance challenge. The dance routine was started by the Angolan dance troupe 'Fenomenos do Semba', who created the Jerusalema dance challenge video in which they danced, holding plates of food in their palms. It brought a feel-good factor throughout the world at an otherwise very gloomy time. Covid-19 brought out the commonality between all human beings. We were all similarly affected and came together to support each other. Covid-19 has made us realise that the most important things in life are music, love and friendships, not material things.

New skills

People had to find ingenious ways of keeping busy during the lockdown, so cooking and baking challenges commenced amongst family groups in the absence of eating out. Julie's family urged each other to bake cakes and make pastries, then post the photos on our WhatsApp group page. There were also online cookery and social skills courses. The situation was so stressful that Julie's son introduced her to mindfulness/relaxation techniques on a website which was very helpful in calming people down. Many online meet-up groups, like Julie's writing group, met on Zoom to share poetry or prose and friendship. The widows' and widowers' group Julie belongs to also joined the Zoom age later, where they could all meet and support one another.

The African and Caribbean Women's Association was a lifesaver in filling the time and connecting with others. The group met every week for a long time until the lockdown was eased; then these became fortnightly meetings because schools were re-opened, some of the members had children in school, and some people resumed work. The meetings allowed the members to connect and support one another through the difficult days. They also came up with many coping strategies to get through the isolation. Some people took to gardening in the summer, while others went for walks. But as the weather changed to winter, Julie was introduced to 'walk at home' videos on YouTube: a 30-minute walk a day gives one about 3,000 to 5,000 steps on the Fitbit app. Walking at home is excellent physical exercise.

Zoom

Many people had not heard of Zoom before the pandemic, even though it existed, but today Zoom has been a real live saver for many people and businesses. It was suitable for video chats and meetings. The help of social media, the internet, online courses, and Zoom made one able to stay connected with others. The pandemic brought Zoom to public awareness. People could work from home because of Zoom, and many businesses have found it cost-saving. Whereas one would have travelled once or twice a week to meetings, now they could hold the meeting on Zoom. Community groups have been able to keep meeting on Zoom, which has helped to engage with those who are elderly or isolated.

Zoom helped in bringing people together and keeping them connected. In fact, it has made members of the same families who live on different continents able to connect with one another at a level not possible before. Julie has siblings in different African countries and states in the USA, but Zoom has made it possible for them to come together and celebrate. This ability to connect has been exciting and gives them something to look forward to as they can see one another on screen. Zoom events connected people all over the world during the pandemic. One day Julie had a Zoom mass at the Vatican at 8.00 a.m., then a cousin's funeral thanksgiving service in Nigeria at 12.00 noon, a wedding anniversary in London at 5.00 p.m., and a family meeting with siblings on three different continents at 8.00 p.m. Zoom provides infinite opportunities for connecting. There were Zoom weddings and birthday parties, book launches and even funerals. Long after the coronavirus has been eradicated or controlled, Julie is sure that Zoom is here to stay in a way that was not possible before Covid-19. It cannot replace human contact, but it brings people together from far and wide in a physically impossible way.

Updates

Julie's curiosity made her volunteer for the Oxford/ government Covid-19 research project last October that will last a year. On the team's first visit, blood and swabs of her throat and nostrils were taken. Unfortunately, Julie never received the result of that first test. She did everything possible to get the antibody result, but it did not happen. It was clearly stated in the research information that it aimed to determine if one has had Covid-19 before, and volunteers were to receive all the results of all the tests. There was about a six-week lull, and the research was resumed, but there was no other blood test, only weekly swabs which all returned negative for Covid-19. Only blood tests can be used to detect antibodies to the virus.

Julie has bombarded the helpline with phone calls, and they always promised to forward her requests to the relevant department, but she is still waiting for the first result. After her illness in Nigeria in March 2020, she will always wonder if she has had Covid-19 and survived it. Unfortunately, she will never know the answer to that question as she is now triple vaccinated, unless that first blood test can be unearthed.

A new virus strain was causing new concerns. The government rolled out Covid-19 vaccines in December

2020, so there was light at the end of the tunnel. Some people were sceptical of the efficacy and safety of the vaccine, but the majority clung to the hope that scientists had got it right and awaited their turn to receive the vaccine.

The news media reported that Captain Tom died on 2 February 2021 after a coronavirus diagnosis. . The Queen and the Prime Minister Boris Johnson led tributes to Sir Tom and described him as a national inspiration and a beacon of hope. The flag flew at half-mast at 10 Downing Street for Sir Tom. He was a national hero.

The first case of the omicron variant of the coronavirus was announced on 24 November 2021 by South Africa. It soon quickly spread around the whole world. The UK decided to list some countries as red list countries, including Nigeria. Once again, Julie was stuck in Nigeria unless she came back on time, then she would have had to quarantine over Christmas, incurring a cost of £2,330, in a crappy hotel, so she extended her travel date by two weeks to explore a way around the rule. Fortunately for her, the government removed Nigeria from the red list, and she was able to return early to the UK to spend Christmas with her family. However, the airline doubled the ticket price when hr return date changed, and she had to amend the ticket.

Covid sunshine: A day in Covid-19 lockdown

Another day has dawned. It is 10.30 a.m., and Julie is still in bed. It is no surprise as she went to bed at 1.45 a.m., woke up at 4.15 a.m., stayed awake for three hours reading a book and then closed her eyes again. She got out of bed, pulled both sides of the blackout curtains, and looked out of the window. It was a beautiful sunny morning with more sunshine to come. The scene was eerily quiet. Usually, she could hear the schoolchildren at playtime screaming and screeching on the school playground behind the houses. The public park behind the school and the houses stretch out underneath her windows. There are rows of terraced houses across the road, and not a single soul to be seen about this morning. The air was still with no wind, no swaying of branches of full ripe-green trees, no birds singing, no voices of children and no families with babies in the park, so the swings and seesaws were all empty.

The only sound Julie could hear this morning was her daughter's voice and her 2-year-old grandson crashing his trains and cars downstairs. Their noises were punctuated by the bleeping sound of the reversing bin lorry outside, and then the postman rang the doorbell to alert the household to parcels delivered. Parcels were now dropped at the doorstep, and the homeowner was alerted by the doorbell. There were no hand-to-hand deliveries and no signatures on books. Looking at the empty streets from her window was a stark reminder that normal life was on hold, despite the sunshine; it felt like a distant dream today. There were very few cars on the road, no caravans, or cars with canoes on the roof, no cars with bicycles standing on the roof, which always intrigued her, and no people teeming about: some driving, some walking in a hurry, some jogging and some just strolling.

Later in the day, a few couples, some with buggies and some singles, could be seen out on their walk. The sunshine was infectious, so Julie went for a walk too. Her daughter decided to come along with the baby in a stroller. A couple and their kids were playing football on a nearby field. On the way back, they were sunbathing, which was now a 'crime'. We stopped to admire the colourful flowerbeds; flowers were in bloom, and Julie recognised daffodils. The flowers were a good reminder of normal life as she always stood to admire beautifully trimmed gardens while out walking.

There were some elderly couples about; they were not power walking but strolling, just breathing in the fresh air and taking in the beautiful scenery. There was an array of well-trimmed gardens on the path. One could also hear lawnmowers doing their thing. Families were out on their walk, and some were gathered in their back garden around barbecues, a little semblance of normal life as we knew it. It all seemed okay but for the two-metre distance between people and the empty streets.

Young joggers were running past, and not-so-young joggers were wobbling along. Julie and her daughter had to walk on the road several times to make way for others with more babies than them on the pavement, obeying social distancing. Others moved down for them, too, when they had no kids and were not elderly. On a positive note, one must mention that people were very courteous to one another, nodding, smiling, and occasionally whispering thank you when you gave them space.

On the way back, Julie and her daughter walked through the centre of the village street and were pleasantly surprised to see the Tandoori shop open alongside the Co-op, the post office and the doctor's surgery. There was a single person here and there. It was good that the 'Stay at home' message was being taken seriously. These extraordinary times required these draconian measures, which hopefully saved many lives in this pandemic.

They got home after an hour to find that Julile's son-in-law and son had come back from work, lit a barbecue, and cooked a selection of burgers, sausages, and chicken wings. They ate them inside the house. It was quite a pleasant surprise. Julie was lucky her daughter and family were stranded there for the entire lockdown instead of the two weeks they had planned to fit their kitchen. Lockdown was announced, all shops closed, and so did all home improvement jobs; some remained uncompleted.

The sunshine is a sign of better things to come. It lifted their mood and motivated them to walk and exercise, which was a positive thing. Tomorrow is another sunny day.

The future 1

We heard or read coronavirus news on TV, social media, and on our phones. Stories about young and old people who, without pre-existing health conditions, contracted the virus and died. The virus is no respecter of persons. It has infected members of the royal family, heads of state, celebrities, and ordinary folk. Many thousands of people died of the disease worldwide, and there is the scenario of those who did not die but have become severely incapacitated with medical conditions they never had before.

This pandemic has revealed a lot of dilemmas. Those who work from home complain of new medical conditions just like those who do not work. It is even worse for those who have lost their jobs. Mental health is the most talked-about condition. People, both young and old, are suffering from anxiety and depression. Weight gain and waist ache from inactivity are also problems that people are experiencing. Some people reported their first attack of migraine during the lockdown. The lockdown has taken its toll.

Life has never been disease-free or problem-free, but this pandemic is an additional burden affecting every aspect of our lives dramatically. Just imagine all the companies that have gone bust and all the workers who have lost their jobs. A few companies have benefitted from the pandemic because they operate online, but most companies and employees have lost out. The high street is not the same without Debenhams and Topshop, Dorothy Perkins, Evans and Wallis and many others, all probably casualties of the pandemic.

In the present climate, talk of the future is tentative and short-term. One has no choice but to take each day as it comes. No one could control the fallout from the pandemic but only try to minimise the impact on us. People are still getting infected; all we can do is obey all the safety requirements and hope that the new vaccines being developed will decimate the effect of Covid-19 on humans and reduce it to something like flu or the common cold. That is what the scientists are hoping for anyway. Many lessons have been learnt for how people should live in the future. One is certainly going to be more humane to realise the connectedness of all humans and how we need to work together. Some people oppress and denigrate others based on colour or economic power. Death does not separate us into economic or social class; these have no bearing on the life hereafter.

There will be more appreciation for the outdoors than being stuck in five-star hotels while on holiday, and people will be less greedy in acquiring wealth and living a simpler life. Some had mortgages too big for their earnings because they were in the rat race trying to impress others and just a little reduction in salary took them over the edge. So, the advice is 'to live within your means'.

Covid-19 brought out the generosity in us, with everyone sharing with their neighbours and food parcels being distributed by companies and individuals. The world may become more compassionate as we realise that life is very delicate and that love matters, friendships matter and family matters more than silver and gold. So hopefully, there will be more communication and generosity between all.

The future 2

Many people now worry about the future in terms of returning to normality as we knew it. One worries about economic security, health security and cultural life. All these concerns have fuelled different reactions in all of us. Many people wonder when they can go away on foreign holidays again, while the priority now is staying alive for others. Tourist destinations and countries will always be there when the pandemic is over.

Julie, like everyone else, has been hit badly by the pandemic. To begin with, Julie worried terribly about her children at the height of the pandemic when there was much more hype about it and its fatal effect on Black people. A good number of the initial wave of coronavirus deaths among hospital workers were disproportionately of BAME people. Julie's children and two sons-in-law are all frontline workers, so it was difficult and fearful for her. Coupled with this fear was a recent diagnosis of some underlying health issues. She counts herself lucky to be safe and well with her children and prays it remains so.

Julie knew some victims of Covid-19, including her 52-year-old cousin who died in London. He may have had diabetes, but it was Covid-19 that killed him. He was asked to stay at home and take fluids and painkillers until it was too late to try any medication to help him. He died 20 minutes after getting to the hospital before any medication could be given.

Julie has taken the resolution to make fundamental changes in her life post-Covid-19. Before now, she worried about many things that she could not change, like who gets sick or does not get sick; she used to worry also about what people thought of her and tried to please everybody. Covid-19 has helped to sharpen her attitude and perspective on life and remind her of one's mortality. Julie has resolved that in the future, she will focus on what makes her happy: do away with toxic relationships and situations and concentrate her energy on the positive things in her life. At 66-plus, there is no better time to wake up to this reality.

FREEDOM

Life is so precious

Preserve at all costs

Freedom is now lost

Lockdown beginning

Loss of human touch

No work. No visits.

No parties. No meetings.

No worship. No outdoor.

Life is frozen in time.

Welcome to lockdown!

Incarcerated!

Ailments multiply!

With close family.

Zoom and online life,

Or lonely confinement.

Mental stress amplified

Lockdown now eases,

Is life unfurling?

Covid-19 a flu?

What price for freedom?

Freedom to touch, hug

Freedom to roam, stare

Freedom to continue

Life's natural cycle!

Patricia Iredia

The sunshine is a sign of better things to come.

Patricia Iredia

Chapter 11

EXTRAS: TEASERS

Just below the surface

Lily was intensely jealous of Lulu. The choice of names by both ladies seems like popular ones in their industry as they sound exotic. Lulu was a very pretty girl who was the centre of attention at every party. Lulu always sweeps into the room with glitter in her fiery red hair as if she owns the room and everything in it. She always has sparkles on her clothes, a flirty smile, and a glint in her eyes reserved only for men. For Lulu, life is about having fun; life is about living without the hassles that come with it. She has practised her skills well to get to this point. With her frizzy hair and chubby contours, it was not easy initially. Now, she is curvy and very slim-built. She used to dance in nightclubs and pubs and has mastered her new art to the point that she does not need to dance anymore. Her presence is enough for the pub owner as she brings a celebrity aura with her and has a cult following fawning over her.

Lulu was not always this glamorous when growing up on the wrong side of town. She grew up in a home with parents who were alcoholics and where drug use was common. Lulu skipped school, smoked, drank alcohol, had a baby at 14, and was coupled with boyfriends that beat and abused her. She dropped out of school and hung out with the wrong crowd, where it was not 'cool' to be smart; otherwise, she would have harnessed her intelligence for better use. By 18, Lulu was an escort and experienced at walking the streets, standing on street corners in skimpy clothes and with cigarettes in hand to create a persona of 'cool'. She had many ugly experiences with drunken men who brazenly assaulted her, so after one horrible incident when an attempt was made to drag her into a car, she decided that walking the streets might not be so safe.

As she grew older, she also discovered that working in nightclubs gave her a better chance of meeting more customers. For starters, she was out of the cold and had some knowledge and censure of the characters with whom she associated. She started as a bartender, then graduated to pole dancing; luckily, she could sing a bit, so she made a good karaoke entertainer. She had a good enough voice to raise the roof in a karaoke contest and found herself being applauded with standing ovations and prolonged whistling. She realised that she was beginning to attract the right kind of attention and was becoming a valued asset to the business, judging by the demand for her presence daily on duty. She was a vibrant and popular employee. The boss discovered that customers came in for her evening entertainment on the pole and her singing and were very disappointed when she was not there.

Things changed for Lulu gradually. Before, only the drunken guys would approach her at the close of the day, but now she could dare to go for the executive-looking men who came in after work to have a pint. By this time, she had changed the colour of her hair from brown to gold to red before deciding to stick with red, and hair extensions made the hair look big and vibrant. That was it; she would keep this colour because she got a lot of compliments.

Lulu knew that everyone at the club looked out for her. They knew who she left with every time. She was clever enough to heed the advice her police coordinator gave her to get off the streets after a vicious attack by a smelly drunk customer who picked her up, refused to pay, left her bloodied, and attempted to kidnap her. Lulu had come a long way from the skinny 18-year-old who first arrived on the scene. Now she was a self-assured lady who knew what she wanted out of life. Anytime she remembered the squalor of where she grew up, Lulu squirmed and shuddered to herself and vowed never to return to that sort of life, the vomit, violent quarrels, and fights. She was far away now, in a big city where she could hide and be anonymous.

It wasn't a perfect new world. It was a dog-eat-dog business, and Lulu always checked out the competition for fear of being upstaged. In this business, there is always a new fresh face turning up to share the limelight or even take over and overshadow the incumbent. Lulu was not ready for that yet; she felt she was still in her prime and could successfully ward off any competition.

When she first met Lily, she appraised her as not a competition. Lulu had at least one advantage over her: she could serenade the men while gyrating her waist around the room. Lily could not sing and was as thin as a stick without any curves to tempt a man. Lily was pretty but needed to build up her confidence. She was still picking up the down and outs who paid a pittance. Now Lulu was picking and choosing and had graduated into the kind of woman that 'decent' blokes kept exclusively on the side for themselves. She had no problem being 'owned' so long as the man could pay all her bills. Lulu graduated from being a floor dancer to becoming a 'Madam' in her own right.

Now, she mentors young runaways on how to settle down in the city and become independent. She weans them out of street life and mentors them to get a job. She was doing good in society, helped by the police, which added to her importance in the community. Some of her girls turned their lives around when they met someone and settled into family life, but not all chose that path. Some quit the streets and took on jobs in shops or clubs. These are not bad girls; most of the time, they are just victims of their circumstances.

Lily had fuzzy brown hair and must dance all night, working for a living. She was quite skinny and dull, looking like she would break, looking quite vulnerable, which is not an advantage in this business. She needed to have a glossy dolly look with the help of make-up and be vibrant and confident to succeed and move up the levels. How can you attract a top executive who wants a sidekick if you look so fragile? They want a strong woman who knows what she wants, who would not wake up tomorrow morning and declare undying love for him when he has a wife and kids at home. She needed to get tough and look it, the look that gives the persona of having no care in the world, solid, discreet, and independent.

Lily had been watching Lulu and knew she had some way to go in that business to get to the next level. She wished she could be like Lulu without a care in the world, the envy of the girls and prize for all the men. Lily thought that life was not fair. Why do some people have it all? Lulu always had a man to fend for her and had no care in the world. She wore beautiful clothes and jewellery, and all the men surrounded her table while she, Lily, was half-naked and turning and twisting around the pole. Only the drunk and beer-bellied men were leering at her. By the end of the evening, these were too drunk even to find their way to the bathroom.

Looking at Lulu and Lili now, it is hard to imagine that they started their lives in the same housing estate. They grew up in a poor neighbourhood together where drugs were common, and kids hung around street corners smoking and drinking, and they got involved intimately with boys too early. Early in life, they learned about 'turf' wars and gang loyalty. In this adult business, like ever before, one must mind whom you tread on. There's always a turf war simmering underneath; for example, it was never deemed acceptable to hit on someone else's man or woman or to give any information to the police about drug pedlars.

Lily had been around the club for months when she decided she was fed up with playing second fiddle to anyone. She needed more money to pay her rent and climb up the rental market. Lily was tired of living in a 'dump' and wanted a nice apartment to go home to after a day's hard work. She knew that she had to add bigger extensions to her hair, dye it bright red and style it into big cascading curls. She went home and practised her walk and a flick of the head. She was going to cut her dancing hours and try the 'celebrity' life. She bet nobody would recognise her in glamorous clothes as the same tacky half-naked girl dancing around the pole, and now she would give herself a chance to find a man who would pay her bills, not one-night stands.

Lulu would recognise her, especially as competition wasn't always welcome by her and the audacity of choosing to be another red-haired girl. Lili wanted it all. It was a big club. 'Surely there's room for another girl to shine?' thought Lily. 'What about the days Lulu cannot come in, especially now that she has bagged herself a regular?' she asked. Lili had worked long enough in the club to have friends, and some of the staff also owed her a few favours. She decided to use her day off to try out her new image.

Johnny always came to this pub at 7.00 p.m. every day on his way from work. As a rule, he gravitated to the right-hand corner, where a group of pub friends assembled to have a drink and play cards. He convinced himself that he was having a bit of fun and not gambling, and that the wife was wrong to think something was wrong with their finances. Johnny always had an eye for Lulu, everybody did, but the competition was just too fierce. He had his luck for weeks until she became bored with him and found a more generous offer. Johnny sat in his usual corner and quickly surveyed the smoky room while trying to attract the waiter's attention. That was when he noticed this 'new' red hair at the bar, smiling across the room at him. He then decided to go and get his drink from the bar instead. He made a beeline for Lily and struck up a conversation.

'Are you new around here?' he asked.

Lily replied, 'I'm only about 9 months old in this part of town,' which was a half-truth with the omission that she was the same dancer that danced on the pole some days of the week. The big hair covered half of her face.

Lulu observed this interaction from the corner of her eyes and was not happy that Lily was daring into her territory.

Johnny was a creature of habit. He would wake up at 6.00 a.m. every day, eat the same breakfast, walk the same route, and take the same train to work. Johnny had done this same job for 30 years and had risen from an office assistant to the company's general manager during this period. He held himself up as an exemplary character, a man of integrity and honour, a 'holier than thou' kind of fellow, so much so that a little flexibility was a *sine qua non* for the employees under him to be happy at their job. It was perhaps surprising that such a disciplined man had allowed himself to pile up the weight recently, and everyone wondered what he was up to after work.

Every day, halfway to his home, Johnny would get off the train and head for the pub. The only time he was flexible was during the closing time at work which made his trips to the pub and what he did afterwards possible. He had told his wife that the nature of his job demanded that he had no precise closing hour. He could always take a client out for a drink or dinner, which often happened, especially in recent months. He was the manager who had to pander to their most important clients and keep them happy. He explained to his wife, Janet, that most deals were sealed at these informal meetings. He, therefore, had two to three hours he did not have to account for every day, and he got more brazen. He walked out of the pub daily with a lady on his arm into the backstreets and a posh, exclusive 'members-only' apartment complex. He had been doing this for years. It was an exclusive club accessible to paying members who used the hotel-style apartments.

One day Johnny's wife, Janet, was out shopping with her friend, Carol, when the friend insisted that they go to the new shopping centre next to the pub that Johnny frequented. Then she suggested that Janet might see her husband in the pub across the street as she had seen him coming out of there a few times before with 'clients'. Her friend, Carol, had a hairdressing salon across the road from the shopping complex and got to hear all the gossip from her customers as usual in salons, especially when they feel that no one knows them, or they do not care who knows their secrets. Carol probably knew something that Janet didn't. She encouraged Janet to pop into the bar to have a drink with her husband before going home; 'it will be a nice surprise', she said.

Janet was initially reluctant, but as she got into her car to return home, she suddenly changed her mind. She decided to look for Johnny in the pub. He might be alone if his 'guest' had left. She missed him at home. She had been quite lonely for the past few months, with Johnny always working late and coming home drunk half the time. He could drink because he did not take the car to work at the city centre office and was lucky to have all his train and taxi journeys paid for while 'working'. She almost chickened out of entering the pub. 'What if he is with an important client?' she thought, then planned that she could always slip away quietly, unnoticed by him.

Janet finally entered the pub. It was a crowded Friday evening, and the usual crowd was all there, not that she would know. When they got there, Janet still believed it must be a corporate outing for Johnny to have been spotted here by 'a friend'. When she could not see him anywhere, she decided to ask if he had been in the pub. She proceeded to ask for Johnny, and it didn't take long for all the regulars to learn that Johnny's wife was looking for him. Judging by her look, clothes, and appearance, you knew this was someone's innocent wife. That was when Lulu decided to break a cardinal rule to become a snitch, which should never happen. As the ancient proverb says, 'There's honour among thieves.' Lulu came up to Janet and whispered in her ear, 'If you go around this building to the apartment block behind, just wait behind the gate for a while, and Johnny will come out.'

So, Janet went around the building and saw the posh apartment block inside a gated compound. Unfortunately, the security house was not manned; it had a secure keypad for entry, so there was no one to ask. Janet became apprehensive but curious, and something made her decide to wait and see if someone would let her in or give her information. So, she waited and was lucky not to have waited too long before she sighted two people coming out of the apartment building. The lady had huge red hair covering half of her face, a very short black leather skirt and very high patent black stiletto shoes. She and the man were leering at each other, happily laughing, with the man's hand enveloping her shoulder as they strolled towards the gate. Janet gasped in recognition, 'What is Jonny doing here, and who is this woman?'

Johnny sighted her simultaneously, his hand dropped from Lily's shoulder, and the smile was wiped off his face in shock. He stopped and became frozen to the spot. Lily looked from one to the other, a bit confused at first, then quickly regained her composure and, with her eyes averting contact with Janet's, walked past her into the horizon, leaving husband and wife behind, staring at each other.

Fantasy

Life had never been more promising. In the current climate of scarce jobs and the disappearance of permanent jobs, anyone with a stable job was very lucky. Then, there was always the dream of juggling the salaried job with some business to augment the family finances, but that always came with additional pressures. Isaac had started a business while working in the UK before going for a stint in the Middle East. He had a stable contract job in the Middle East but was also running an import-export business. His cheques were paid into banks in the UK, so he continued his business with his partners while there. He had a business arrangement with a company in London who were happy to ship medicines like Omega 3 to partners in Lagos.

Isaac was home on holiday in Benin City, Nigeria, where the family were residing. He had just returned from a Lagos trip feeling very energised and hopeful that his business deal was going according to plan. There was excitement in the air, quickly punctuated by shrieks of laughter from one end and a shrill cry for help from the opposite end. The kids were at it again.

'What is it now, fighting again?' to which comes the quick reply from the usual suspect.

'We are not fighting. We are playing,' the children reply.

'Well, it doesn't look so to me, judging by the hot tears I can see from here,' answered Julie.

She placates the little one and quickly turns back to her husband for an update on the journey. The consignment of medicines that he ordered from the UK had arrived safely at the Port of Lagos. He had to make the five-hour drive to Lagos to clear it with customs. Things were never straightforward in Nigeria; one must have a clearing agent who charges an exorbitant price for clearing the goods and demands 'bribes' for customs officials to smoothe the path; according to the agents, the customer could never verify that.

Julie and Isaac reminisced about the first time he tried using a bus as a container to bring goods for sale. The imported vehicle was packed with all kinds of goods. It stayed so long at the Port that it was broken into and emptied of all the goods, including the bus's engine. This theft occurred after the clearing agent had collected all fees and extras and had not cleared the goods on time. Julie and her husband later found out the agent wanted a cheaper shortcut route and had fallen victim to scammers, so he claimed. Isaac lost everything.

The only time he was lucky was when he was shipping a used generator from the UK, and the shippers phoned to say that there had been an accident and that the big second-hand generator was damaged. This accident was a blessing in disguise because the old generator was replaced with a smaller brand-new Lister generator, which was very durable and still works today. The big generator was a bit too big for the space he had, but he had bought it because it was cheap.

On this occasion, the goods were delivered to the correct address in Lagos, and the wholesaler pharmacy collected the medicines and paid in cash, as credit was not allowed. The buyer paid cash before carrying the goods, as a credit plan was previously abused when he had not kept his promise to sell and pay off his debt. Everything had gone smoothly according to plan. The business had gone well, so Julie was very happy.

Julie was cooking Isaac's favourite beef vegetable soup, and mashed yam called pounded yam. She was cooking like for an army because relatives and friends could show up unannounced, and any remnants of the casserole could be kept in the fridge for another meal. She was very excited because she had been promised a 'new' car if all the sale deals went according to plan. Even though

Isaac earned most of the money abroad, it was more prudent to trade with money than make a straight currency exchange. This thinking turns everyone in the diaspora into an importer and exporter. Hard currency is hard to come by, so those who have it maximise their income by trading in goods, usually in collaboration with a local person on the ground. They buy second-hand clothes, televisions, cars, tractor engines, etc., and there's a market for them. It is almost like subsistence farming, the little guys doing their 'one man' business beside the large-scale commercial traders.

This situation is easy to grasp when you understand that most foreigners from third-world countries living and working abroad live double lives. Some might be working abroad while their immediate families stayed behind in Africa. Many working permanently here in the UK have dependent parents, siblings, and extended families to support back home. They often have to help with school fees, medical bills, and the demand for cars (to use as taxis) or buses (to use for hire or transport business) for relatives. How can one cope with that demand and still have any quality life while paying their bills here? There have been instances of those being supported living a more comfortable life than the one doing three jobs to support them. There was the story of someone being supported by his brother who got himself two dependant wives while his brother was working three jobs in America! Sometimes, they build a house for their parents and siblings to replace their crumbling mud houses or to help them quit renting.

Isaac kept his promise to buy her a new car if all the goods were sold, so he bought her a shining 'new' (used) car from the Wharf in Lagos, delivered to Benin two days later. A lot of good things were happening to her at the same time. The following week, they flew off with the kids to London on holiday to visit all the family and Buckingham Palace again. The last time they tried doing Madame Tussauds and the zoo on the same day, they had got to the zoo too late. This time, hopefully, they would go back to the zoo.

Julie had a spring in her step because she was about to launch the 'new' car. She was getting ready to go to her nephew's wedding with Isaac, and as usual, Julie was running late and could hear the continuous beeping of the horn for her to come out. She hurriedly picked up her handbag and tried to rush out of the house but stumbled over her 4-year-old sitting quietly on the floor behind her dressing-table chair. She recovered her balance and hurried out, brushing past the nanny. As she got nearer the car, Isaac started up the car engine and tilted his head to look at her through the car window as she opened the passenger door to get in.

Julie woke up with a jolt. Then she slowly realised that she was lying on her bed. It was all a dream! Isaac had already died; Julie had been a widow for years. She had just relived her life of over 35 years ago.

Chapter 12

PATRICIA'S STORY:

Extract from *New Shoots Old Roots*

This community project was a collaboration between the African and Caribbean Women's Association (ACWA) and Street Level Photoworks in Glasgow. This final material is a transcription from audio interviews.[20]

I am originally from Nigeria; I came to Scotland in 1996 to live with my husband in Stornoway in Lewis, where he was working as a consultant gynaecologist. However, I first came to the UK in 1980, and we lived in Belfast just after we got married. Isaac was a trainee doctor then. In

---

[20] African & Caribbean Women's Association (ACWA), *New Shoots Old Roots*. Glasgow: Independently published, 2015.

Nigeria, I was a civil servant and had just got a job with the Department of Education when we met at Isaac's sister's wedding. Eighteen months later, I was in Belfast! I had two children in Belfast, after which we were all over the place because a trainee doctor is not settled until he is a consultant.

We have lived in London, Wales, and the Middle East.

Then we considered relocating back to Nigeria, so Isaac took a job in Saudi Arabia. The children and I returned to Nigeria but spent all our holidays in Saudi Arabia. That soon lost its attraction, and we returned to the UK in 1996 after Isaac got a job in Lewis, Western Isles. After eight years there, Isaac died of cancer. I was left with the last two of our children at home for another three years until they were old enough to go to university, and we relocated to Glasgow in 2007.

The first impression I had coming to the UK was exciting. I was going to a new country. I had a new husband and a new life – it was exciting and frightening at the same time. I had never left home except to go to the university. I was looking forward to a new life, but when I got to Belfast, the excitement soon wore off! I wasn't used to that lonely life – you are locked in all the time, especially during the Troubles in Northern Ireland. I went to Queen's University as soon as I got there in 1980 to do a postgraduate diploma in Education and made some good friends, but people met up in the pub, not in the home like back in Nigeria. A few classmates would invite me to the pub, so we went there, and we gambled on horses, and yes, that was nice. Those were the good old days!

Stornoway Island was another cup of tea. The first time we got there, it was exciting because I was now coming with five children to Stornoway, and I thought, 'Oh my God, this is the end of the earth!' The people's behaviour was more like home; all the neighbours were very friendly and in and out of each other's houses. We didn't lock our doors; you didn't need a key. I had one key to the front door for 11 years, and you weren't scared that anyone would burgle you or harm you.

Many people had not been that close to Black people, so they probably found it a novelty. One day, as we were coming out of the post office, we came face to face with two men, and one of them almost had a heart attack. He said, 'Jesus of Nazareth!'

His friend had to apologise on his behalf, and we just laughed and said, 'Okay, it's okay.'

He said, 'Jeez, where are you from?'

We said, 'We come from Africa. We live here!'

We were the only Black African people on the island for a long time until another doctor with three children came to work there. They didn't stay for long before they were off again because he was temporary staff. So, most of the time, it was just us, and we were the first Black African people ever to own a house in Stornoway.

Everyone was nice; neighbours, teachers, and all. The occasional problem would rear its ugly head. We couldn't believe such blatant racism/discrimination could happen in a packed school hall. I can't understand why some people would do some of the things my children experienced. I can understand with little kids. I mean, kids will be kids. It is the adults I could not understand – why my daughter and my son would win a competition for the school that was so important that the headteacher and another senior teacher accompanied them and another child to an awards ceremony in Edinburgh. They came back on the prize-giving day. Every little achievement/participation is acknowledged on the school's prize-giving day, and medals are awarded. So, we kept waiting for it to be announced, and then the MC mentioned that the headteacher had just returned from Edinburgh with '*some children*' who won '*some competition*'. To this moment, it wrenches my heart when I remember how the children reacted. We were stunned that their names were not mentioned. My son said with tears in his eyes, 'Dad, I am very sorry that I didn't get any medal.' And I don't know what happened because the headteacher was embarrassed. My husband phoned up the next day to complain and said, 'My children have names. It is a shame that children who brought honour to the school were not acknowledged.' She was very apologetic and came back to the house with medals. That was just one incident; most of the time, it was OK.

Initially, the weather was a bit of a shock; we don't have winters in Nigeria. We have two seasons, rainy and dry. It was rainy, cold, and dark in Lewis a lot of the time. It goes dark early in winter but also has longer daylight in the summer. You get used to it after a while. When we had visitors, they'd say, '*Oh my God!*'

It became normal for me. I loved the shore because I had never lived on the coast before. I loved the ferry terminal and walking along the promenade – it had spectacular views. There were lochs and hills; it was a good life. First and foremost, the children were safe and able to thrive.

I quickly learnt from when I was first married to stop thinking about African food because the ingredients were too hard to find. When I married, I was 25 years old and living in Belfast in 1980; you couldn't find any African ingredients except rice and stew, so you just got used to whatever was in your environment. I got a Marks and Spencer cookery book and would make Lancashire Hot Pot and the children's recipes from school – lasagne, potatoes, casserole, mincemeat, pasta, and various cakes. In Stornoway, we used to eat haggis every Burns Night. I adapted to the local food. I didn't have chillies for 11 years, and I didn't care! When I came to Glasgow in 2007, African food was everywhere. These days food is international.

I was a full-time housewife until the death of my husband. I volunteered with the Council Day Care Centre, and the boss saw me one day and said, '*Why don't you go work in the home with adults with learning disabilities? It's near your house.*'

So that was how I started, and I worked there for almost three years. When I first moved to Glasgow in 2007, I worked for myself privately from home, but it was so lonely that I wanted human contact apart from family – my children were at university, and when they returned home, it was laptop and phone. We would talk on the phone sometimes in the same house! I joined the African Caribbean Women's Association (ACWA) to meet other African women and make new friends. Today, I am the current Chair of the organisation and am privileged to be involved in this book project. I am also proud that I re-

registered at the University and have completed my PhD in Educational Psychology. There is also church and other members for activities. I worked as a carer and later as a support worker, but it was very irregular hours. I had to travel to Nigeria a lot, so I had to give it up. My four daughters were getting married one after another! And my ageing mother was getting frail, and she was a wheelchair user, so I was going backwards and forwards to Nigeria.

Then came the dilemma when all my children left home: I was alone for the first time in my life. I'd been thinking, *'What shall I do now? Will I stay in Scotland or go back to Nigeria?'* The answer was simple. I did test out living there for three months at a time, and I find it increasingly difficult to think I can live there permanently now. Here, I am lonely, but the tap is flowing (no borehole), there is light (no generators), and no iron bars on my doors and windows. I can watch TV peacefully and get in my car; my children are nearby. I have grandchildren coming for sleepovers, and I babysit a lot. Nowadays, I keep myself busy by joining/volunteering with various charitable organisations, social clubs, church activities, amateur writing, and family.

So, looking at the pros and cons of each place, I would say overall, growing up in Stornoway was a positive experience for my children; there was more positive discrimination because they were the only Black African children. The secondary school was very good; it allowed my children to grow. They all did very well, and all had the support they needed. I can proudly say, I have two doctors, two nurses and one pharmacist/medical student.

I try not to focus on racism; there are good and bad people everywhere. I do not deny that institutional racism exists in the UK, but there is discrimination in Nigeria too. If you are a Muslim or Christian, if you are from one region and want a job in another, you may have a problem.

We raised our children to be very positive and go-getters, not to be negative, blaming the system or racism if things don't work out. My advice for my children was always, 'Go for it. Go for whatever you want. Don't let anybody or anything stop you.'

A REMOTE PLACE

Here we come to Isle of Lewis
The remotest place I'd lived in.
The weather changeable and wild
With daylight long in the summer
And darkness long in the winter
The storms can blow your roof away.

There, I had the best sleep ever
There, memories to last forever
There, the worst pain I'd ever felt
As death knocked out our Patriarch
The whole town rallied round with love
Neighbours, friends, came to the rescue

The house was filled with gifts of food
A helping hand mowing the grass
A helping hand clearing gutters
A helping hand with house minding
A helping hand with childminding

Sad but wonderful memories

The most vivid of memories
The kindest place I'd ever lived
A remote place yet not so far
Africa, million miles away
Isle of Lewis a flight away
Near or far, loving hearts connect.

Patricia Iredia

ABOUT THE AUTHOR

Dr Patricia Osarhiemen Iredia was born in Benin City, Nigeria, in the 1950s and first relocated to the United Kingdom in 1980 after she got married. She holds a PhD in Educational Psychology and worked as a civil servant and an education officer in Nigeria before relocating to the United Kingdom.

In the UK, she lived in Northern Island in the 1980s during the Troubles and had five children in Northern Island, Wales, and London between 1981 and 1989. She relocated to Nigeria with her family for some years but came back in 1996.

She finally settled in the Isle of Lewis with her late husband, a consultant gynaecologist in the local hospital. He later died there after a brief illness, and she had to move again when the last child left home, this time to Glasgow. She is a mother to four daughters and one son, and grandmother to eleven grandchildren.

Patricia has been an education officer, a homemaker, and a support worker. She is currently a businesswoman and a volunteer, helping women and children in various sectors, including currently being a Panel Member of Children's Hearing, Scotland.

She is a Forum member of the Scottish Ethnic Minority Older People Forum, Scotland, a former Chair and member of the African & Caribbean Women's Association, a member of African and Caribbean Elders Scotland, and a current treasurer of the Glasgow Women Voluntary Sector Network.

She loves her writing group in Glasgow, UK, where she goes weekly to be with other budding writers and enjoys sharing stories and poetry.

Keep the faith
Keep the light
Be the light

Patricia Iredia

REFERENCES

African & Caribbean Women's Association (ACWA). *New Shoots Old Roots*. Glasgow: Independently published, 2015.

BBC News. 'President Obama tells young to reject cynicism' (23 April 2016): https://www.bbc.co.uk/news/uk-36119829 (accessed: 1 September 2022).

BBC News. Updated: https://www.bbc.co.uk/news/uk-scotland-53076269 (accessed: 18 June 2022).

Booth, R. 'Racism rising since Brexit vote, nationwide study reveals' (20 May 2019). *The Guardian*: https://www.theguardian.com/worl/2019/may/20/racism-on-the-rise-since-brexit-vote-nationwide-study-reveals (accessed: 21 October 2020).

Britannica. 'Barack Obama: Facts & Related Content': https://www.britannica.com/facts/Barack-Obama (accessed: 29 June 2022).

Bulman, M. 'David Lammy says treatment of BAME groups in criminal justice system has got 'considerably worse' since his review' (26 March 2019). *The Independent*: https://www.independent.co.uk/news/uk/home-news/david-lammy-review-bame-criminal-justice-black-ethnic-minority-a8840306.html (accessed: 10 January 2022).

Daly, M. and McKay, C. 'Sheku Bayoh: Why did my brother die in police custody?' (18 January 2021).

Grierson, J. 'Windrush scandal: UK's Windrush scheme begins refusing people deemed ineligible for citizenship' (21 September 2018). *The Guardian*: https://www.theguardian.com/uk-news/2018/sep/21/uk-windrush-scheme-begins-refusing-people-ineligible-for-citizenship (accessed: 10 January 2021).

Imonikhe, T. 'Oba Ewuare 11: A quintessential monarch at 66' (18 October 2019). *The Guardian*: https://guardian.ng/opinion/oba-ewuare-ii-a-quintessential-monarch-at-66/ (accessed 18 March 2021).

King Jr, Martin Luther. 'Letter from a Birmingham Jail [King, Jr]' (16 April 1963). African Studies Center – University of Pennsylvania: https://www.africa.upenn.edu/Articles_Gen/Letter_Birmingham.html (accessed: 26 March 2021).

Koutonin, M. 'Stories of Cities #5: Benin City, the mighty medieval capital now lost without trace' (18 March 2016). *The Guardian*: https://www.theguardian.com/cities/2016/mar/18/story-of-cities-5-benin-city-edo-nigeria-mighty-medieval-capital-lost-without-trace (accessed 20 October 2021).

Nwaubani, A.T. 'Remembering Nigeria's Biafra war that many prefer to forget' (15 January 2020). BBC News: https://www.bbc.co.uk/news/world-africa-51094093 (accessed: 4 September 2021).

Office for National Statistics. 'Updating ethnic contracts involving the coronavirus (COVID-19), England and Wales: deaths occurring 2 March to 28 July 2020' (16 October 2020): https://www.ons.gov.uk/peoplepopulationandcommunity/birthsdeathsandmarriages/deaths/articles/updatingethniccontrastsindeathsinvolvingthecoronavirusCOVID19englandandwales/deathsoccurring2marchto28july2020 (accessed: 21 August 2021).

Osei-Oppong, M. *For the Love of Teaching in Education: The Anti-Racist Battlefield in Education*. Peaches Publications, 2020.

Porter, L. 'All of The Times Barack Obama Professed His Love for The First Lady' (26 October 2020). Essence.com: https://www.essence.com/celebrity/black-celeb-couples/best-barack-obama-quotes-michelle-obama/#81869 (accessed: October 2021).

UK Parliament. 'Analysis of the EU Referendum results 2016' (29 June 2016). House of Commons Library: https://commonslibrary.parliament.uk/research-briefings/cbp-7639/ (accessed: 28 February 2022).

Weale. S. 'RACE: Most Black British children report experiencing racism at school' (29 October 2020). *The Guardian*: https://www.theguardian.com/world/2020/oct/29/most-black-british-children-report-experiencing-racism-at-school (accessed: 20 October 2021).

Wikipedia. 'Nigerian Civil War':
https://en.wikipedia.org/wiki/Nigerian_Civil_War#Nigeria
n_offensive (accessed: 23 February 2021).

Wikipedia. 'The Troubles':
https://en.wikipedia.org/wiki/The_Troubles (accessed:
15 March 2021).

Printed in Great Britain
by Amazon

34119934R00159